My Kitchen, Your Table

General Notes
The cup measurements in this book are US cups.
When using stock cubes and powders, avoid those with preservatives
and too much salt. Instead, choose those with only natural products.

Published by
Landmark Books Pte Ltd
5001 Beach Road,
02-73/74
Singapore 199588

Landmark Books is an imprint of
Landmark Books Pte Ltd

ISBN 978-981-4189-60-6

Printed in Singapore

My Kitchen, Your Table

Audra Morrice

◦LANDMΔRK◦BOOKS◦

To my family and friends for supporting me,
and to the people that come in and out of my life for teaching me.

CONTENTS

Introduction

My journey in the world of food began as a child. I was born in Singapore on 19 February 1970. My mother, born in Sibu, Sarawak, in East Malaysia, is Chinese of Hock Chew descent. My father was Indian, Singaporean by birth, with parents from Madras and Pondicherry in the south of India. Anyone could've guessed that being born into a family of such a cultural mix, the food we ate was undoubtedly going to play a big part in my life.

The Seventies in Singapore was colourful, to say the least. I often think I am one of the lucky ones who experienced much of the old Singapore and have seen the growth and development of this culturally-rich country into what it is today. Despite the beautiful, modern outlook, Singapore still preserves much of its diversity through its multicultural people – and with that comes a genuine mix of great food. The essence of what makes Singapore such a wonderful place to have grown up in is in everyone's kitchen, the recipes that have been passed from generation to generation and the pride that each and every family takes in preserving their family's secret recipes. The influences of my family and friends, the food of Singapore and my travels since I was a young child have moulded me and my cooking.

You could say that my mother has been my biggest inspiration in many ways – as a mother, a wife, a person, and a cook. In her eyes, everything was achievable, so long as we applied ourselves. Mom moved away from home to further her studies, specialising in dressmaking and design in Hong Kong, and later, London. She came from a timber-merchant family with nine siblings, five girls and four boys, all of whom were either brilliant cooks or had a great love for food. For them, searching out the best food was one of life's greatest pleasures.

Growing up, I spent much time with my mother's side of the family. I remember digging for clams along East Coast beach with my cousins. With buckets full of fresh and beautiful shells, we'd walk back to the house and my aunt would cook them up. They were the freshest clams you would ever taste. What joy we had, sitting around the dinner table picking them open with our fingers and sucking them dry of all their flavours – a subtle mix of black beans and lots of chillies. Simply divine! Every dinner, my mother and her sisters cooked like they would for a celebration. There was no doubt about their generosity of heart. It's typically

Chinese to always have an abundance of food, and this celebration of abundance is very much a part of who I am and how I cook.

The frequent visits to see my grandparents in Kuching, Sarawak, was also filled with generous meals, the table always ladened with delicious dishes. The beautiful old-style, four-storey shophouse had a mezzanine dedicated to the kitchen – how I dream of having such a place today!

My mother told me that everything she knows about cooking she learnt from my grand-mother. Thankfully, the genes didn't skip a generation. I always thought my grandmother was somewhat of an "Empress Dowager", strict as she was about dining etiquette. However, there was a deeper message in her actions. She taught us all that by showing respect at the dinner table, we respected the cook and the food that we ate. Till today, my kids are reminded not to eat with their elbows on the dinner table and not to leave any food on the plate. A wise lady she was.

For breakfast, while the little ones had wonton wrappers cooked till soft in a light broth, the bigger kids would walk several blocks to a *kopitiam* or coffee shop for the best Kuching laksa. After a bowl of this mouth-watering, spicy coconut broth, there was not a care in the world – just a feeling of satisfaction. It's no surprise then that laksa is one of my favourite dishes. I have now created my own recipe that has all the flavours of fresh aromats, the pungency of dried shrimp and the richness of coconut (see page 34).

When I was growing up, home-cooked meals were the women's forte while sniffing out the best eats were the men's. So, needless to say, we were often out with my uncles eating the best fish balls, sotong or cuttlefish balls, Kuching egg noodles and more.

We often think of soup in the Western world to be creamy or chunky. Soup in the East is often broth-based, made from a slow-cooking process to create clarity and depth of flavour. I was the "Soup Queen", often drinking bowls and bowls of beautiful, slow-brewed broth sometimes flavoured with pork bones, other times cooked with beef shin, preserved Szechuan mustard greens or salted cabbage and, the best of all, a hearty steamed black chicken with Chinese herbs. Oh, the satisfaction from drinking a hearty bowl of soup is the greatest feeling! In this book, I share some recipes for home brews

LEFT: *My brother and me with Mom and grandmother.*
RIGHT: *Digging for clams in Singapore.*

that will stand tall on their own or can be cooked with noodles for a more substantial meal.

It's no surprise then that I was never the problem child when it came to mealtimes. As an infant, toddler, young child, teenager and now an adult, I ate almost everything that was placed in front of me. You could say I was every parent's dream child when it came to eating. Now both you and I know that that is a BIG deal!

Despite a glorious upbringing in Singapore and getting to know my Chinese heritage well, I often pondered over my Indian heritage. This might explain my obsession with South Indian food and chillies.

My paternal grandparents died very early on, and I never met them. My father told me that after leaving the Indian Army, my grandfather worked for many years as a waiter and butler to the British governor of Singapore, then later as an assistant cook to General Yamashita, the man who captured Singapore during World War II, and then back for the British (Lord Mountbatten!) after the war was over. How amazing it would've been to have exchanged recipes and cooked with him and my grandmother. Dad shared with me that my grandmother was a true legend at making one of my absolute favourite Indian dishes – appom, a coconut-based, thick pancake that was served with either sambar, a savoury lentil-based vegetable broth, or orange-tinged sugar. It's mouth-wateringly divine! I am still trying to master the art of making it! Thankfully, every trip back to Singapore brings me to a little South Indian vegetarian restaurant in Little India which satisfies this craving.

My desire to travel to India to explore and experience my Indian heritage remains intact. Research, talks, discussions and invitations are all there, but I still can't believe that I have yet to go. All I know is when I do step foot in India, emotions will stir as I see what life might have been like for my grandparents. I can't wait!

Sadly, Dad passed away a year before this book was published. He would have been ever so proud to see that his family and food memories play a big part of my life. Memories of dad and his stories will forever remain close to my heart.

In the late Eighties, studies took me to Christchurch in South Island, New Zealand. There, I was exposed to a whole new food culture and an incredibly fresh range of produce. You might ask what some of my favourite activities were. Topping the list was picking fruit – cherries and apples. Being able to taste the extraordinary, fresh NZ green-lipped mussels and

TOP: *Grilling prawns for an episode of Tasty Conversations.*
RIGHT: *In a Singapore wet market with Mom.*

12

savour the freshest raw salmon straight out of the icy glacial waters – what more could you ask for!

I moved to Sydney in the late Nineties, married, and had two beautiful children. This is where I live today. My time in Australia has taken my love for food and cooking to a higher level. After spending almost 20 years in telecommunications winning multiple sales awards, and facing the realities of life's pressures and responsiblities, I finally, with full support from my family, mustered up the courage to give Masterchef Australia a go. I wanted to explore if food was where I wanted to be for the rest of my life. Today, I look back with a big smile, no regrets, and only excitement that I get to wake up each day and do what I love – cook! For my kids, this is one of the biggest life lessons I could ever share with them – be passionate, love what you do, and if you believe in it, go for it!

My travels around the world has given me much appreciation of life, food and people. From cooking in the most humble and basic open-fire kitchen in Cambodia to being amongst the most sought-after seafood in the world at the Tsikiji Fish Market in Tokyo, and travelling on rickety bikes to local markets in Hanoi, each experience has created new ideas and new perspectives for me. I'd like to think that I am evolving as a cook, taking memories of my upbringing and my travels to create food that satisfies the soul. I am truly excited!

My immersion into the world of food and the opportunity to write this book is a dream come true. Through these recipes, I share with you my childhood, my family, my travels and my life. I share with you absolutely everything I love to eat. I hope it will bring to your home as much joy as it has to mine, and will give you reason to cook for each and every occasion.

Food doesn't need to be classified or put into boxes. Food is not just something to fill an empty stomach – it's a way of getting to know yourself, your neighbours and the world we live in. Through food, we learn about culture, and through culture we broaden our minds and become more accepting, and through these culinary experiences, we live a better life.

To life, and its never-ending journey of exploration and experiences of food!

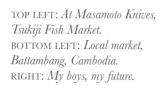

TOP LEFT: *At Masamoto Knives, Tsukiji Fish Market.*
BOTTOM LEFT: *Local market, Battambang, Cambodia.*
RIGHT: *My boys, my future.*

Growing-Up Years

We all have memories of childhood. Mine are steeped with food, family and traditions. The dishes that my mother used to cook for health – her special home remedies – for celebrations and for everyday meals made a big impression on my life as a child and now as an adult. You don't forget the flavours and smells from a kitchen. I am still being influenced by Mom's kitchen and how she cooks. That was where my life of food began.

Steamed Black Chicken Soup

SERVES 2-4

This soup is a walk down memory lane, bringing me back to my early childhood. My mother, like most Chinese mothers, believes that soup is a cure for all ills. The black chicken has dark-coloured skin and flesh but white feathers and has a natural sweetness that makes this soup not only wholesome but delicious.

Mom used to steam this with goji berries and a host of Chinese herbs in an old claypot over low charcoal heat all day, adjusting the heat as she needed. The result? A sweet, scrumptious soup that truly fed the soul. There are lots of brews. Go to your local Chinese herbal specialist and ask for this mixture, then add a little dong sum and ginseng for a more nourishing brew!

1 whole black chicken,
  washed and cleaned
1 tablespoon kei chi
  (goji berries, wolfberries)
30 g (1 oz) wai san
  (wild Chinese yam)
30 g (1 oz) fook ling
  (Poria mushroom)
30 g (1 oz) leen chi (lotus seed)
30 g (1 oz) see sut (Euryale seed)
2 sticks dong sum (Codonopsis
  root) and a little ginseng
  (optional)

Scald the chicken in hot water to remove any impurities. Rinse under cold water.

Place the chicken in a deep ceramic or enamel bowl slightly larger than the chicken, then add all the herbs and enough water to just cover the chicken. Place a rack at the bottom of a pot and put the bowl on the rack. Pour in hot water to halfway up the sides of the bowl. Cover the pot with a lid. Bring to the boil, then reduce to low-medium heat and steam for 2 hours.

NOTE: Dried Chinese herbs can be found in Chinese medicine or herbal shops at your local Chinatown. If you can't find these scrumptious black chickens, a small 800 g (1.7 lbs) chicken or spatchcock will suffice.

Beef Shin and Preserved Szechuan Mustard Greens Soup

SERVES 4

I love the combination of beef and Szechuan mustard greens. The saltiness of the greens work so well with the beef to make a rich, flavoursome beef broth. You can use all beef instead of beef bones. For a hearty meal, add some blanched flat rice noodles and choy sum and serve with the tender beef, mustard greens and soup.

600 g (1.3 lbs) beef shin
300 g (10.5 oz) beef bones
250 g (9 oz) Szechuan mustard
  greens, washed well, thickly
  sliced
2 knobs (20 g, 0.7 oz) ginger,
  peeled, thickly sliced
1 large onion, peeled, wedged

Trim the fat off the beef shin, retaining the muscles and tendons. Cut the beef into large pieces across the grain.

Place the beef and bones in a pot filled with water. Bring to the boil, remove from heat and drain.

Place the beef, bones and all other ingredients in a clean pot and fill with about 8 cups of water. Bring to the boil, lower to simmer and cook for 2 hours, or 45 minutes in a pressure cooker.

Beef Curry Puffs

MAKES 24

Curry puffs come in all sorts of pastries. Making them with shortcrust pastry is by far my favourite. This is another regular snack I grew up eating. I spent a few years living in Kuala Lumpur as a young child and the best curry puff I ever tasted was at the Lake Club in KL. It was really spicy, chilli hot and incredibly moist and tasty, not to mention massive. And as a kid, anything that was big was good!

SPICY BEEF FILLING

600 g (1.3 lbs) lean minced beef
300 g (10.5 oz) potatoes, peeled, diced (½ cm, 0.2 in), boiled until just tender, drained
1 stalk curry leaf or to taste
3 cloves garlic, peeled, grated
1½ knobs (15 g, 0.5 oz) ginger, peeled, grated
1 large Spanish onion, peeled, finely diced
½ cup finely chopped coriander roots and stems
2½ tablespoons curry powder
1 teaspoon ground cumin
1 teaspoon sweet paprika
1 teaspoon ground coriander
1 teaspoon chilli powder
1 tablespoon tomato paste
2 teaspoons salt
2 teaspoons sugar
½ cup roughly chopped coriander leaves
3 tablespoons oil

SHORTCRUST PASTRY

400 g (3.2 cups) plain flour
Pinch of salt
200 g (7 oz) cold unsalted butter, cubed
100-150 ml (about ½ cup) ice-cold water with a dash of white vinegar

1 egg for egg wash

To make the filling, heat 3 tablespoons of oil in a non-stick frying pan over medium heat. Add the curry leaves and fry for 20 seconds until lightly blistered. Add the garlic, ginger, onion and coriander stems and roots. Fry for 2-3 minutes, stirring frequently until the onions soften and are slightly golden around the edges. Increase to high heat, add the beef and cook until brown, stirring and chopping with a wooden spatula to remove lumps.

Add all the dry spices, tomato paste, salt and sugar and mix well. Add the potatoes and 2 tablespoons of water, stir well, reduce to low heat, cover and cook for a further 5-8 minutes until the potatoes and meat are really tender. You may have to add some water. Note the mixture should be wet but not sauce-like. Adjust seasoning with more salt to your taste. Add the chopped coriander leaves and toss well. Remove from heat and set aside to cool. This can be prepared a few days beforehand.

For the pastry, place the flour and salt in a food processor and blitz for 10 seconds. Add the butter and pulse until the mixture resembles coarse breadcrumbs. With the motor running, add cold water in a slow, steady stream until a dough comes together. The amount of water required will largely depend on your butter and the climate. In warmer climates, you may not need as much water.

Turn the dough out onto a clean surface. Pat into a round disc, wrap with cling film and refrigerate for 20-30 minutes.

Preheat the oven to 180°C (356°F). Line two baking sheets with greaseproof paper.

Roll the pastry out to about 2 mm (.07 in) thickness between two sheets of plastic. Starting from one end of the dough, cut out discs using a 10 cm (4 in) or larger round pastry cutter. Fill with 1½ tablespoons of filling, fold the pastry over and press the edges to seal. Then press and twist the edge to get a rope-like finish. Brush lightly with the egg wash and bake the curry puffs for about 30 minutes or until lightly golden and crisp.

Char Siu Bao

MAKES 10

I can comfortably proclaim that my mother makes the best bao in the entire world! She has set me up to literally baulk at steamed buns made purely with baking powder, the sort that sticks to the top of your palate! Remember that you should always use plain or low gluten flour to make bao.

MARINADE
1 teaspoon hoisin sauce
1 teaspoon dark soy sauce
2 teaspoons light soy sauce
½ teaspoon sesame oil
¼ teaspoon white pepper
¼ teaspoon five-spice powder
3 teaspoons sugar
2 tablespoons water

FILLING
200 g (7 oz) char siu or roast
  pork, diced into ½ cm pieces
4 dried shiitake mushrooms,
  rehydrated in water, trimmed,
  finely diced
2 tablespoons oil
2 cloves garlic, peeled, finely
  chopped
1 knob (10 g, 0.4 oz) ginger,
  peeled, finely chopped
1 medium Spanish onion,
  peeled, finely diced
¾ teaspoon cornflour, mixed
  with 1 tablespoon water to
  form a slurry
1 sprig spring onion, diced
1 tablespoon crispy shallots

DOUGH
300 g (2 cups) plain flour or
  low-gluten flour
2 tablespoons caster sugar
1½ teaspoons dried active yeast
1 tablespoon oil

Make the marinade by mixing together the hoisin, dark soy, light soy, sesame oil, white pepper, five-spice powder and sugar with 2 tablespoons of water.

To prepare the filling, heat 2 tablespoons of oil in a wok. Fry the garlic, ginger and onion over medium heat until softened. Add the char siu and mushrooms and stir to combine. Reduce the heat to low, then pour in the marinade, stirring to combine. Stir in the cornflour slurry and cook for about 1 minute, mixing well. Turn the heat off, stir in the spring onions and crispy shallots. Allow to cool.

To make the bao dough, place the flour in a mixing bowl. Create a well in the middle and pour in the sugar, yeast, oil and about ¾ cup of lukewarm water. Mix together to form a sticky dough. Pour out onto a lightly floured surface and knead until smooth. Dab with a little flour and return to the mixing bowl. Cover with a damp cloth and leave in a warm place until the dough doubles in size. This will take at least 40 minutes to 1 hour. In colder climates, this might take a lot longer.

Fill the steamer pot with water, remove the steamer racks, cover, and bring to the boil. Cut out 5 x 5 cm (2 x 2 in) squares or discs of greaseproof paper. Set aside.

Pour the dough out onto a lightly floured surface. Roll into a long, snake shape and divide equally into 10 pieces, kneading each well and placing them in order.

Roll a portion of dough out into a 3 mm (0.1 in) thick disc and place a heaped teaspoon of filling in the middle. Gather the edges up to the top to seal by pleating, pinching and turning. Dab the bottom with some flour, place on a piece of greaseproof paper and put the bun onto the steamer rack. Repeat with the rest of the dough and leave for 20-25 minutes or until the dough has risen slightly. Steam for 20 minutes or until fluffy and cooked.

Water will collect under the lid of the steamer, so be careful not to tip it onto the buns when removing the lid. To avoid this, wrap the lid with a thin cloth prior to steaming.

Mom's Spiral Pastry with Shredded Spiced Roast Chicken Filling

MAKES 20

My mother is the "Queen of Pastries". I suspect that's where my love for pastries came from. I spent countless hours watching her work on pastries, constantly improving them until she was happy with the result. Pastries are one of those things you have to spend time on. The more you do it, the better you understand how they work and the better you get at it.

This method requires a little effort but it's worth it. Whilst deep frying creates the perfect morsel, I've given the option of baking it. Note the difference in the composition of the oil dough for deep frying and baking.

SPICED ROAST CHICKEN FILLING
2 roast chicken breasts, shredded
1 stalk curry leaf
3 cloves garlic, peeled, grated
1 knob (10 g, 0.4 oz) ginger, peeled, grated
1 large onion, peeled, halved, finely sliced
1 small bunch fresh coriander, washed, trimmed, roots and stems finely chopped, leaves separately chopped
1 tablespoon curry powder
1 teaspoon ground cumin
Salt to taste
Pinch of sugar
Squeeze of lemon juice
Oil
2 large hot green chillies, finely sliced on the diagonal

DOUGH FOR DEEP FRYING
Water dough
300 g (2 cups) plain flour
10 tablespoons water
2 tablespoons vegetable shortening or oil

Oil dough
150 g (1 cup) plain flour
4 tablespoons vegetable shortening or 5 tablespoons oil

Start by making the filling. Heat 3 tablespoons of oil in a non-stick frypan over medium heat. Add the curry leaves and fry for 20 seconds until lightly blistered. Add the garlic, ginger, onions, coriander stems and roots, green chillies and fry until the onions are slightly golden around the edges. Add the curry powder, cumin, salt and sugar. Cook for 2 minutes then add in the shredded chicken, squeeze in the lemon juice and chopped coriander leaves. Toss to mix. Taste and adjust accordingly if more salt or sugar is needed for your taste. Remove from heat and set aside to cool.

To make the water dough, place the flour in a large mixing bowl, add the water and oil or shortening and mix to form a dough. Knead lightly, wrap with cling flim and rest for 20 minutes.

To make the oil dough, place the flour in a mixing bowl, add the vegetable shortening and mix to form a dough. Knead lightly, wrap with cling flim and rest for 20 minutes.

On a lightly floured surface, roll the water dough out into a large rectangle. Roll the oil dough into a rectangle about a third the size of the water dough and place it in the middle third of the water dough. Fold over the water dough to encase the oil dough. Roll into a long rectangle. Fold the dough into thirds, make a 90° turn and roll the dough out again into a long rectangle. Repeat this process once more. From the short end, roll snugly into a Swiss Roll form and refrigerate for 10 minutes. Slice the roll into 20 pieces of 3 mm (0.1 in) thickness. Lay the dough flat between two sheets of plastic and use a small rolling pin to roll the pastry out to a disc of about 2 mm (.08 in) thick and slightly larger than 10 cm (4 in) in diameter. Use a 10 cm or larger ring pastry cutter to trim the discs neatly. Repeat with remaining dough.

DOUGH FOR BAKING
Water dough
300 g (2 cups) plain flour
10 tablespoons water
2 tablespoons vegetable shortening
　or oil

Oil dough
225 g (1½ cups) plain flour
6 tablespoons vegetable shortening
　or 7½ tablespoons oil

Fill each piece of dough with 1½ tablespoons of filling. Fold the pastry over the filling and press the edges to seal. Then press and twist the sealed edges until you get a rope-like finish.

To deep fry, preheat the oil to 170°C (338°F). Deep-fry in batches until golden. Drain on paper towels and serve warm.

To bake, preheat your oven to 180°C (356°F). Brush lightly with egg wash and bake the curry puffs for about 30 minutes or until lightly golden and crisp.

Chicken Rice
SERVES 4

Chicken Rice is all about the rice. The poached chicken is almost secondary. Master the rice and the chilli relish and you'll have happy diners. What makes the rice so delectable and delicious is the addition of rendered chicken fat. I suppose it's like what duck fat is to roast potatoes. Don't skimp, there is no low-fat version!

2 cups (400 g, 14 oz) jasmine
　or long-grain rice, washed and
　drained
Chicken fat from the cavity of
　the chicken, roughly chopped
　(see Soy Sauce Chicken, page 46)
1 tablespoon oil
4 cloves garlic, peeled and
　crushed
2-3 slices ginger
375 ml (1½ cups) homemade
　or good quality, store-bought
　chicken stock
1 pandanus leaf, knotted
　(optional)
1 teaspoon salt

Heat both the oil and chicken fat in a medium saucepan over medium heat. Render off as much of the fat as possible. The fried fat should be lightly golden and crispy when all the fat has rendered off. Remove and discard the fried fat or keep for topping.

Add the garlic and ginger and fry for 1 minute. Put in the drained rice and fry for a couple of minutes until each grain is well coated. Add the stock, pandanus leaf and salt and bring to the boil. Stir well and reduce the heat to as low as possible. Cover and simmer for 8-12 minutes or until the rice is cooked. Fork through and add extra salt if required. Cover and let it rest for 10 minutes.

Chicken rice should not be mushy. If anything, it should be cooked to al dente and the grains should be separated, so be careful not to add too much water and don't skimp on the chicken fat.

Serve hot with my Soy Sauce Chicken (page 46) and Fresh Red Chilli Relish (page 167).

NOTE: Chicken fat can be frozen. So, if you're roasting a chicken but not using the fat from the cavity, wrap it up tightly in cling film and freeze until needed.

Pot Stickers

MAKES 30

Yum! Yum! Yum! Pot stickers were the first dumplings I ever made with my mother. It is so incredibly delicious and something I now make for my family quite often. It's really one of the best Chinese creations, combining simple and inexpensive ingredients and applying techniques that only comes with practice and patience. I've provided a cheats option using store-bought gow gee wrappers but I encourage you to make the real thing!

POT STICKER DOUGH
300 g (2 cups) plain flour
¾ - 1 cup hot water

FILLING
200 g (7 oz) minced pork or
   chicken
2 cloves garlic, peeled, finely
   grated
½ knob (5 g, 0.2 oz) ginger,
   peeled, finely grated
2 leaves Chinese cabbage,
   white or Savoy cabbage
2 stalks spring onions, finely
   chopped
1 small bunch chives, finely
   chopped (optional)
1 small brown onion, peeled,
   finely chopped

MARINADE
1½ tablespoons soy sauce
½ tablespoon oyster sauce
1 tablespoon Shaoxing wine
½ tablespoon sesame oil
½ teaspoon white pepper
½ teaspoon sugar
1 tablespoon cornflour

DIPPING SAUCE
½ knob (5 g, 0.2 oz) ginger,
   peeled, finely julienned
1 tablespoon dark vinegar
   or Chinkiang vinegar
½ tablespoon light soy sauce
½ tablespoon dark soy sauce
Pinch of sugar
½ teaspoon chilli bean sauce

Plain flour
Vegetable oil

Gently wilt the cabbage in a microwave, then finely chop and squeeze to remove as much liquid as possible. In a bowl, mix the meat, garlic, ginger and marinade. Combine well then add the chopped cabbage, spring onions, chives, onion and combine again. Set aside in the fridge.

For the dough, prepare a small bowl of water and a tray dusted lightly with flour. Place the flour in a mixing bowl. Make a well and pour in ¾ to 1 cup of hot water, stirring with chopsticks to form a slightly sticky mass. Turn out onto a lightly floured surface and knead until smooth and elastic. Place the dough back in the mixing bowl, cover with a damp towel and rest for at least 10 minutes.

Roll the dough into a long snake and divide into 30 equal pieces. Knead each into a ball. Roll a ball into a 1 mm (.03 in) thick disc. Turning frequently in a clockwise direction while rolling will help create a round shape. Flour well to avoid sticking. Put 1 teaspoon of filling in the middle of the wrapper, leaving a clear edge. Fold the wrapper over the filling. Pinch the edge at the top of the semicircle. Make three pleats on the right side of the semi-circle towards the middle, then another three pleats from the left side of the semicircle also towards the middle, pressing firmly to seal as you pleat. This will create the slightly crescent shape of the pot sticker. Dab the dumpling in flour and place on the flour-dusted tray. Repeat with remaining dough and filling.

Boil a kettle of water. Heat a large non-stick pan over medium heat. Drizzle with 2-3 tablespoons of oil.

Place the dumplings neatly facing the same direction in the pan, leaving a little space between dumplings. Cook till the bases are lightly seared, then pour enough hot water to halfway up the sides of the dumplings, cover and simmer until the water has fully evaporated and the dumplings are golden and crisp on the base. Remove.

Make the dipping sauce by mixing all the sauce ingredients. Serve with dumplings.

Mom's Hock Chew
Stir-Fried Crab with Eggs

SERVES 4

When we think of Chinese food, a handful of typical and common dishes come to mind. However, if I had to name all the dishes of the cuisine, I really wouldn't know where to start and finish. Chinese food differs from region to region. Mom is of Hock Chew descent and the cuisine of her dialect group has specialties like this one. It's light and all about the flavour of the crab. The crab is cooked first, then tossed together with fresh aromats and then finished off with eggs. Whilst the crab is the centrepiece, the eggs cooked with the spring onions and chillies are just as delectable. You can just imagine the meals I have had with this wonderful dish at the centre of the table!

1 kg live crab (1 large mud crab or equivalent in medium-sized crabs)

Cornflour for dusting before deep-frying

4 cloves garlic, peeled, finely chopped

1 large knob (20 g, 0.7 oz) ginger, peeled, sliced thinly

3 large red chillies, sliced on the diagonal

2-4 stalks spring onion, cut into 6 cm (2½ in) lengths

2 tablespoons premium light soy sauce

3 tablespoons Shaoxing wine

2 tablespoons chicken stock

¾ teaspoon coarsely-ground white pepper

¾ teaspoon sugar

2 eggs, lightly beaten

Oil for deep-frying

Prepare the crab humanely (see below for tip). To cook the crab, you can either steam, pan fry or deep fry it.

To steam, place the crab in a steamer and cook until all the flesh has turned opaque and the shell orange. Timing will depend on the size of your crab.

To pan-fry, heat 4 tablespoons of oil in a large wok over medium-high heat and cook, tossing a few times until the crab has turned orange and the flesh is opaque.

To deep-fry, heat the oil in a wok to 180°C (356°F). Dust the crab lightly with cornflour and fry until just cooked – the shell should be orange and flesh opaque.

Mix the soy sauce, Shaoxing wine, chicken stock and sugar in a small bowl. Set aside.

Heat 2 tablespoons of oil in a wok. Over high heat, fry the garlic, ginger, chillies and spring onions for 30 seconds. Return the crab to the wok and toss. Deglaze with the soy, wine, chicken stock mixture, pepper and sugar. Toss to combine, then drizzle in the eggs around the crab. Allow the eggs to set slightly, then fold over the crab, no more than 4 to 5 times. Remove from heat and serve immediately.

NOTE: To prepare a live crab for cooking, leave it tied up in a freezer for about 1 hour. If it's a large crab, it may take a little longer. This basically puts the crab to sleep. Then place the crab in the sink, remove the strings, pull the V-shaped flap and lift off the entire top shell. Clean the insides well, particularly near the mouth, removing all the dead man's fingers (these are obvious) and run it under water to clean out the guts. If it's a female crab, keep the eggs in the shell for the dish. Chop the crab in half, then into quarters. The pincers should be lightly crushed with the back of a knife.

Zhu Bi Png (Glutinous Rice)

SERVES 4-6

Sticky rice is one of those dishes that I would always have at my primary school tuckshop. Their version was called in Cantonese, Lor Mai Gai where marinated chicken and shiitake mushrooms were placed at the bottom of a dish topped with glutinous rice, then steamed. When you turn it out onto a plate, the meat appears on top and the juices from the meat and marinade would permeate the sticky rice. Mom's version, which we called by the Hokkien name Zhu Bi Png, is unbeatable with lots of really delicious ingredients added to it. She would always make a huge dish but it was never enough for me! I am delighted that this has become one of my children's favourite one-dish meals.

2 cups (400 g, 14 oz) glutinous rice

3 cloves garlic, peeled and finely chopped

30 g (1 oz) dried shrimp, rinsed, soaked in water for 30 minutes, drained and finely chopped

30 g (1 oz) dried shiitake mushrooms, rehydrated in water, drained, finely sliced

1 medium Spanish onion, peeled, finely diced

2 carrots, peeled, finely diced

200 g (4.2 oz) lean pork or chicken thigh fillets, thinly sliced into strips

1 lap cheong (Chinese sausage), thinly sliced on the diagonal (optional)

2 stalks spring onion, washed, trimmed, finely chopped

Oil

PORK MARINADE

2 teaspoons oyster sauce

1 teaspoon light soy sauce

$\frac{1}{2}$ teaspoon white pepper

1 teaspoon Shaoxing wine

$\frac{1}{2}$ teaspoon sesame oil

1 teaspoon tapioca flour

SEASONING

1 teaspoon light soy sauce

3 teaspoons oyster sauce

$\frac{1}{2}$ teaspoon white pepper

$\frac{1}{2}$ teaspoon sesame oil

Wash and soak the glutinous rice in water for at least 2 hours or overnight. Drain before use.

If you do not have a steamer, fill a wok or a large pot half full with water, cover and bring to the boil. Place a rack at the bottom of the wok and prepare a ceramic dish to sit comfortably on the rack and still have room for the steam to circulate with the lid on.

Mix the pork and marinade in a mixing bowl and leave for at least 10 minutes.

In a separate wok or large deep-frying pan, heat 2 tablespoons of oil over high heat and fry the pork until lightly brown. Remove and set aside. Lower the heat slightly, add another 2 tablespoons of oil, then the garlic, dried shrimp, mushroom, onion, carrot and lap cheong and fry until fragrant.

Add the drained rice and pork, the soy sauce, oyster sauce, pepper and sesame oil. Stir well and cook for a further 2 minutes. Transfer to the steaming dish and steam covered for 30 minutes or until the rice is cooked through. Note that the rice should not be mushy, but rather, cooked and still holding its shape.

Szechuan King Prawns

SERVES 4

My family and relatives gave me many nicknames as a child; they were all names that related to the love I had for various foods. So, I was "The Soup Queen" and also "The Prawn Queen". I absolutely love prawns, particularly cooked with their shells in tasty, sticky sauces. Mom always bought king prawns from the market and cooked it in this rich, dark vinegar, soy and chilli marinade. Just thinking of it still makes my mouth water. Master this dish and you will be "The Prawn Queen" in your family. All the preparation needs to be done prior to cooking as once you start, it all happens very quickly.

500 g (1.1 lbs) king prawns
¼ teaspoon Szechuan peppercorns
¼ teaspoon five-spice powder
¼ teaspoon coarsely ground white peppercorns
½ teaspoon sugar
¼ teaspoon sea salt
1 teaspoon cornflour or tapioca flour
2 teaspoons water
3 cloves garlic, peeled, thinly sliced
1 knob (10 g, 0.35 oz) ginger, peeled, thinly sliced
1 large hot red chilli, sliced thickly on the diagonal
1 medium Spanish onion, peeled, halved and thickly sliced
2 stalks spring onion, washed, trimmed and cut into 5 cm (2 in) lengths
2 tablespoons oil

MARINADE
2½ tablespoons black vinegar
1 tablespoon dark soy sauce
1 tablespoon Shaoxing wine
1 tablespoon raw sugar
¼ teaspoon coarsely ground Szechuan peppercorns
¼ teaspoon coarsely ground white peppercorns
¼ teaspoon sesame oil

To prepare the prawns, use a pair of kitchen scissors to trim the whiskers and cut down the backs and devein. Place in a mixing bowl.

In a medium frying pan, dry roast the Szechuan peppercorns over medium heat for 2 minutes or until fragrant. Remove from the heat and set aside to cool. Grind in a mortar and pestle.

Mix the prawns with the five-spice powder, Szechuan pepper, white pepper, sugar and salt. Massage in and set aside in the fridge.

To make the marinade, mix all the marinade ingredients with 2 tablespoons of water in a small bowl. Taste. It should be mildly salty with a touch of sweetness. Set aside.

Mix the cornflour with the water and set aside.

Heat 2 tablespoons of oil in a wok or large frying pan over high heat. Add the garlic, ginger, chilli, onion and spring onion and fry for 2 minutes until the chilli starts to blister.

Add the prawns and pan fry until three-quarters cooked. Add the marinade and cook for a further 2 minutes. The high heat will help the sauce thicken quickly and caramelise. Add the cornflour slurry and toss till the sauce has thickened and is glossy.

Serve immediately.

NOTE: If you really loathe the idea of peeling prawns during a meal, remove the shell of the prawns before cooking but keep the head and tail on as they add flavour to the dish. Or, at a stretch, use large, peeled prawn cutlets.

Laksa

SERVES 4

Give me a bowl of laksa anytime and I'll be happy. It's one of the greatest dishes ever created in Asia and presumably one that will continue to melt the hearts of many around the world. I have eaten so many different versions of laksa from a really young age, might I also add, for breakfast mostly! I love my laksa rich and spicy. Master the technique of separating the oil from the coconut milk and you're there. All I can say is, thank you, thank you, thank you to the clever people who came up with this dish!

Unless you are using a mortar and pestle, I find it easier to make a big portion of laksa spice paste and freeze the remaining for other recipes (such as Laksa Roast Chicken, page 39) or until you have another laksa craving.

1 chicken, cleaned
4 tablespoons laksa spice paste (page 160)
1 knob (10 g, 0.35 oz) ginger, peeled and sliced thickly
4 cloves garlic, bruised and skinned
4 stalks spring onion
30 g (1 oz) dried shrimp, soaked in water, drained and ground
750 ml (3 cups) chicken stock (reserved poaching liquid) or good quality store-bought
1 teaspoon sugar
1 teaspoon salt or to taste
8 dried beancurd puffs, sliced into thirds
200 g (7 oz) fish cake, thickly sliced
1 cup (250 ml, 1 cup) coconut cream
250 g (9 oz) fresh rice noodles or equivalent of dried thick rice noodles
1½ cups beansprouts, tailed, blanched
12 medium prawns, shelled, deveined, poached until just cooked, sliced into half
Laksa leaves, finely sliced
2 limes, cut into wedges

To poach the chicken, fill a medium saucepan a little larger than the chicken with enough water to just cover the chicken. Place the ginger, garlic and spring onion in the saucepan, cover, and bring to the boil. Lower the chicken into the saucepan ensuring it is submerged in the poaching liquid. Bring to the boil, then reduce the heat to a very light simmer and cook for 20 minutes. Remove from the heat and let the chicken cool in the stock. When the chicken is cool enough to handle, remove the meat from the bones and shred. Reserve the poaching liquid. For this amount of laksa, you probably need meat from only a quarter of the chicken, but a good laksa needs a rich stock from a whole chicken. Keep the rest for my Chicken and Crispy Noodle Slaw (page 151).

Take 4 heaped tablespoons of laksa spice paste (page 160). Add the dried shrimp to the paste in the saucepan and fry for 5 minutes.

Add the chicken stock, sugar and salt.

Add the dried bean curd puffs, fish cake and coconut cream, pressing the beancurd puffs into the soup. Bring to the boil and immediately turn off the heat. Taste and adjust seasoning to your taste. If you are using store-bought chicken stock, taste before adding any salt as the stock might already contain enough salt.

Blanch and drain the fresh rice noodles. If using dried noodles, boil until al dente. Rinse under cold water to remove excess starch and drain. Serve the noodles in a bowl, ladle over the laksa gravy with some tofu and fish cake, top with beansprouts, prawns, shredded chicken, laksa leaves and lime.

NOTE: You can leave the prawns whole. Simply add them to the laksa gravy and remove when they're just cooked.

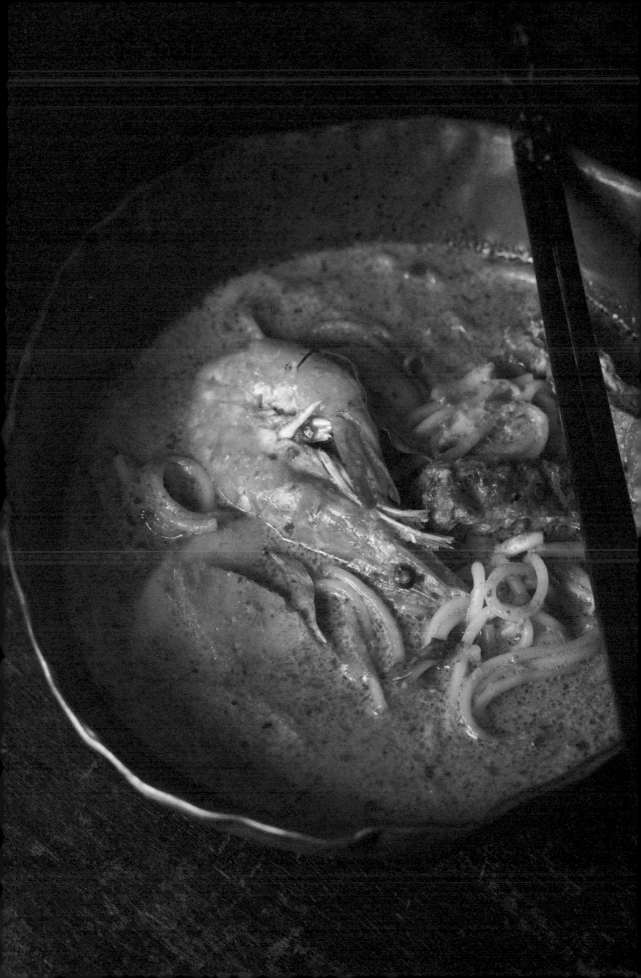

Claypot Snapper

SERVES 6-8

Claypots spell wholesome goodness. You know that everything that's cooked in a claypot will just be a pot of gold. My mother used to make this with the head of Ikan Kurau (Threadfin Herring). If you're not into fish head, then use cutlets as fish fillets are a little too fragile for this dish. Also, the fish bones really help to give flavour. Best of all, it's a one-pot wonder and really simple to make.

600 g (1.3 lbs) king snapper
   cutlets, bone in
1 teaspoon white pepper
1 teaspoon Shaoxing wine
½ teaspoon light soy sauce
Plain flour for dusting
Oil for shallow frying

4 cloves garlic, crushed, skinned
1 knob (10 g, 0.35 oz) ginger,
   peeled and sliced
2 tablespoons oyster sauce
1 tablespoon Shaoxing wine
4 cups chicken stock
½ teaspoon white pepper
50 g (1.7 oz) dried shiitake
   mushrooms
4 cups water

350 g (12 oz) choy sum (Chinese
   mustard greens), washed and
   cut into 6 cm (2.5 in) lengths
100 g (3.5 oz) shimeji mushrooms
100 g (3.5 oz) pearl mushrooms
150 g (5.3 oz) inoki mushrooms
375 g (13 oz) fresh tofu, deep
   fried until golden

3 stalks spring onion, sliced into
   4 cm (1½ in) lengths
Crispy shallots

In a large wok or frying pan, heat about 1 to 2 inches deep of oil to about 180°C (356°F).

Rub the fish with the white pepper, Shaoxing wine and light soy sauce. Dust lightly in flour. Gently lower the fish into the oil and fry until one side is almost cooked and lightly golden. Turn over and cook the other side. Drain on paper towels.

Place a large, seasoned claypot over high heat, add the crushed garlic, ginger, oyster sauce, Shaoxing wine, chicken stock, white pepper, shiitake mushrooms and water. Bring to the boil. Lower the heat to medium, then add the choy sum, mushrooms and tofu to one side of the pot. Place the fish on the other side of the pot, cover and cook until the fish is cooked through. Sprinkle with crispy shallots and spring onions. Serve hot with steamed rice.

NOTE: If you buy a traditional claypot, you will need to season it. First soak it in water, then fill it up with water and heat it over low heat. If you don't have a claypot, just use a large stove-proof casserole dish or saucepan.

Laksa Roast Chicken

SERVES 6-8

My mother came up with this idea and I absolutely love it. I often make a large batch of laksa paste and freeze them in portions. Then, when I need it, I pull one out of the freezer, thaw and use. This dish is insanely good and a really easy one to prepare.

1.5 kg (3.3 lbs) chicken
¾ cup laksa spice paste
  (page 160)
1½ cups coconut cream
1 teaspoon sugar
1 teaspoon salt
2 heaped tablespoons desiccated
  coconut, dry pan fried until
  dark golden
3 tablespoons oil
Squeeze of lemon juice

Butterfly the chicken by cutting through the middle of the backbone from the neck to the tail. Flatten the chicken out with the palm of your hands. Using a sharp knife, score the chicken across the legs, thighs and breasts. Set aside.

Heat an ovenproof, wide-bottom saucepan over medium-high heat. Add 3 tablespoons of oil, then the laksa spice paste and fry for 2-3 minutes. Include the coconut cream, sugar, salt, fried desiccated coconut and ¼ cup of water and cook for a further 2 minutes.

Lower the heat to a simmer, place the chicken skin-side down into the saucepan, basting the sauce over the entire chicken. Cover and cook for 20 minutes. Turn the chicken over, add another ¼ cup of water, cover and cook for a further 20 minutes, basting twice.

Preheat the oven to 180°C (356°F) with the grill setting on. Finish off the chicken in the oven for 5-10 minutes or until the top is golden and a little charred.

Remove from the oven, cover loosely with foil and rest for 5-10 minutes before serving.

NOTE: If you prefer a dish with more spice paste, simply increase the amount of laksa spice paste.

Black Bean and Chilli Clams

SERVES 4

This dish really takes me back to my childhood days when we dug for clams along the beaches of the east coast of Singapore. With buckets and spades digging away, we would get so excited whenever anyone found any clams. Foraging for your dinner was definitely the way to go! My aunt would cook our findings back at her house with a delicious black bean and chilli sauce and the rest of the evening would be spent picking at the shells and devouring the clams.

900 g (2 lbs) clams
1½ knobs (15 g, 0.5 oz) ginger
3 cloves garlic, crushed, skin removed, finely chopped
1 medium (120 g, 4 oz) Spanish onion, peeled, finely diced
2 large long, hot, red chillies, finely diced
1 tablespoon fermented black beans
Pinch of sugar
2 tablespoons Shaoxing wine
1 stalk spring onions, diced
3 tablespoons oil

Soak the clams in lightly salted water for 1-2 hours. This will encourage them to purge out all the sand and impurities from within them.

Heat 3 tablespoons of oil in a wok over high heat. Add the garlic, ginger, onion and chillies and fry for 1 minute. Add the fermented black beans and sugar. Fry for 30 seconds, then add the clams and toss. Deglaze with the Shaoxing wine. Cover with a lid and steam until the clams open. Add the spring onions and serve immediately.

NOTE: You can substitute clams for pipis. They are equally delicious!

Dry Indian Masala Chicken

SERVES 4

Mom had several chicken curry recipes and she always received amazing compliments for this one. Its richness comes from a combination of whole and ground spices cooked with garlic, ginger and onions that are shredded or grated rather than blended to give texture. You can create a version with more sauce by adding coconut milk or yoghurt to it. Doing it the South Indian way, the spice mix is first made into a wet paste by adding water. The versatility of this recipe also allows you to marinate the chicken in the spice paste and grill it over a barbecue.

1.5 kg (3.3 lbs) whole chicken, cleaned and cut into 12 pieces

SPICE PASTE
4 heaped teaspoons good quality curry powder
1 teaspoon ground coriander
1 teaspoon garam masala
$\frac{1}{2}$ teaspoon ground cumin
$\frac{1}{2}$ teaspoon ground black pepper
$\frac{1}{2}$ teaspoon ground turmeric
1 teaspoon sweet paprika
$\frac{1}{2}$ teaspoon chilli powder (optional)

3 green cardamoms, crushed slightly
1 (8 cm, 3 in) stick cinnamon
5 whole cloves
1 stalk fresh curry leaves
3 cloves garlic, peeled, coarsely grated
1 knob (10 g, 0.35 oz) ginger, peeled, coarsely grated
2 large onions, peeled, halved, finely sliced
1 tablespoon tomato paste
3 large hot green chillies, sliced on the diagonal
$\frac{1}{2}$ teaspoon salt
$\frac{1}{2}$ teaspoon sugar
2 slices lemon
$\frac{1}{4}$ cup oil

To make the wet spice paste, in a small bowl, mix the curry powder, coriander, garam masala, cumin, black pepper, turmeric, paprika and chilli powder with 2 tablespoons of water.

Heat a medium-large saucepan with $\frac{1}{4}$ cup of oil over medium heat. Add the cardamoms, cinnamon stick, cloves, curry leaves and fry for 30 seconds. Then add the garlic, ginger, onions and wet paste and fry until fragrant and the sliced onions have softened. Mix in the tomato paste.

Add the chicken pieces and toss until they are sealed and well coated in the spice paste. Turn your heat down to low and simmer with the lid on. To keep the chicken moist and to prevent burning, add a tablespoon of water at a time as required until the chicken is almost cooked. Mix in the green chillies and cook until the chicken is cooked and coated generously with the sauce. Season with sugar and salt.

Remove from the heat, squeeze in the lemon juice and stir in the lemon slices.

Serve with steamed rice.

NOTE: For a version with more sauce, grate both onions and cook as above. Add 250 ml (1 cup) of coconut milk or 120 ml ($\frac{1}{2}$ cup) yoghurt after the chicken has been nicely sealed and coated with the spices and simmer until cooked through.

Chinese-Style Chicken Stew

SERVES 4

I learnt to cook this dish over the telephone. Frequent calls to my mother while I was in university in New Zealand asking for recipes was not uncommon. This is really delicious, simple and quick to put together – ideal for a midweek dinner.

1 kg (2.2 lbs) whole chicken, cleaned, fat from cavity removed, chopped into 16 pieces
2 tablespoons oyster sauce
1 tablespoon Shaoxing wine
1 tablespoon light soy sauce
½ teaspoon white pepper
1 teaspoon cornflour or tapioca flour
3 cloves garlic, crushed, skinned
1 knob (10 g, 0.35 in) ginger, peeled, crushed
1 large Spanish onion, peeled, cut into wedges
1 large carrot, peeled, cut into bite-sized chunks
2 celery sticks, cut into bite-sized chunks
8 dried shiitake mushrooms, rehydrated
1 cup button mushrooms
2 stalks spring onion
1 tablespoon oyster sauce (optional)
1 teaspoon cornflour or tapioca flour
2 tablespoons oil

Marinate the chicken pieces with the oyster sauce, Shaoxing wine, soy sauce, pepper and cornflour. Set aside to marinate for at least half an hour.

In a large saucepan, heat 2 tablespoons of oil over high heat. Add the garlic and ginger and fry for 1 minute. Add the chicken pieces, reserving any remaining marinade. Cook until nicely browned.

Add the onion, carrot, celery and shiitake mushrooms along with ½ cup water. Cover and bring to the boil, then reduce the heat to low-medium and cook until the chicken is almost cooked.

Add the button mushrooms and spring onions and cook for a further 5 minutes. Taste and adjust the flavours. Add the tablespoon of oyster sauce if using and more cracked white pepper if you wish. When you are happy with the flavours, mix the cornflour with 2 tablespoons of water and stir it into the pot. If you prefer more sauce, you can add up to ¾ cup water but adjust the flavours with a teaspoon or so more of oyster sauce.

Serve hot with steamed rice.

Soy Sauce Chicken

SERVES 6-8

Go to a Singapore Chicken Rice stall and you usually have a choice of white poached chicken or soy sauce chicken. The only difference is soy sauce chicken has been bathed in soy sauce. As a young child, I would look for every opportunity to eat Chicken Rice on our Sunday lunch out. You'd easily see me lining up for Soy Sauce Chicken Rice with extra chilli.

Instead of poaching the chicken first, my Mom tosses and turns the chicken carefully in a wok filled with a thick braising liquor. The result? Mouth-watering, delicious soy sauce chicken or tao you kuay as we call it in Hokkien. Inheriting her method, here's my recipe.

1.8 kg (4 lbs) whole chicken, cleaned, excess fat from cavity removed and set aside

POACHING LIQUOR
8 cloves
1 (10 cm, 4 in) cinnamon stick
2 star anise
2 stalks spring onion, washed, trimmed and halved
6 cloves garlic, peeled and crushed
2 knobs (20 g, 0.7 oz) ginger, peeled and crushed
1-2 teaspoons light soy sauce (optional or to taste)
3½ tablespoons good quality dark soy sauce
250 ml (1 cup) water
2 tablespoons raw sugar
2 tablespoons oil

Heat 2 tablespoons of oil in a wok over medium-high heat. Add the cloves, cinnamon, star anise, spring onion, garlic and ginger and fry for 1 minute. Include the light soy sauce if using, the dark soy sauce, water and sugar. Bring it up to the boil. Adjust to taste. If the sauce is too salty for you, dilute with a little more water.

Place the chicken, breast-side down, in the wok. Cover, lower the heat to low-medium and cook for 20 minutes, basting the chicken once, both inside the cavity and over the chicken. Turn the chicken over (be careful not to break the skin) and cook covered for a further 20 minutes, basting the chicken once, both inside the cavity and over the chicken and again at the end. You may need to turn the chicken on either side to ensure the legs and thighs are cooked through. To test, run a skewer through the leg joints. If the juices run clear, the chicken is cooked.

Remove the chicken and allow it to rest for 20-30 minutes before serving. For a thicker gravy, reduce the sauce slightly (Keep in mind that it will thicken as it cools.) Strain through a sieve before serving.

Chop the chicken Chinese style and serve with the gravy, my Fresh Chilli Relish (page 167), Ginger and Shallot Relish (page 169) and my fragrant Chicken Rice (page 25).

NOTE: I find it easier to use a wok to cook this as the natural curve of the wok provides more depth and allows the chicken to soak in the sauce. If you don't have a wok, use a deep saucepan that is just a little wider than the chicken and increase the cooking time to ensure it's cooked through.

Nonya Chicken Curry
SERVES 4

Ask me what my favourite curry is and this would have to be it! I love Nonya cuisine. The use of aromats create such complex and delicious flavours like no other cuisine. Thank goodness for those intermarriages in the early 17th century between the Malays and Chinese which brought the best of both cuisines together.

1 kg (2.2 lbs) whole chicken, cut into 12-14 pieces
5 small potatoes (240 g, ½ lb), peeled and halved

SPICE PASTE
1 large Spanish onion, peeled, cut into wedges
15 long dried red chillies, soaked in hot water, drained, roughly chopped
2 long hot fresh red chillies, roughly chopped
1 knob (10 g, 0.35 oz) fresh turmeric or 1 teaspoon ground turmeric
1 knob (10 g, 0.35 oz) galangal, roughly chopped
1 knob (10 g, 0.35 oz) ginger, peeled, roughly chopped
3 cloves garlic, peeled
3 candlenuts
1 teaspoon (10 g, 0.35 oz) blachan (shrimp paste or Thai gapi), wrapped in foil and toasted in a dry pan over low-medium heat for 2 minutes or until fragrant

2 stalks lemongrass, white part only
2 tablespoons ground coriander
4 tablespoons oil

1 pandanus leaf, tied into a knot (optional)
3 kaffir lime leaves
2 cups (500 ml) coconut milk
1-1½ teaspoon salt or to taste
½-1 teaspoon sugar

In a mortar and pestle or food processor, grind the onion, chillies, turmeric, galangal, ginger, garlic, candlenuts and blachan to a paste.

Heat 4 tablespoons of oil in a large pot, add the spice paste and lemongrass and cook on medium heat until fragrant (about 4-5 minutes). Add the ground coriander and cook for a further 3 minutes.

Put in the chicken pieces, pandanus and kaffir lime leaves. Stir until well coated, then add the potatoes and coconut milk. Stir well and cook until both chicken and potatoes are tender. Season with salt and sugar. Be careful not to break up the potatoes when stirring.

Soy-Braised Duck

SERVES 4-6

My mother used to cook this with extra duck feet that her butcher would throw in free of charge. We would sit at the dinner table and chew through the entire duck, dipping it in a fresh red chilli relish (page 167). I reckon this dish truly solidified my love for duck! It's cooked in a very similar way to the Soy Sauce Chicken (page 46) but with the addition of five-spice and a richer dark soy braise.

1 whole duck, cleaned

1 teaspoon soy sauce

½ teaspoon Chinese five-spice powder

POACHING LIQUOR

8 cloves

1 (10 cm, 1 in) cinnamon stick

2 star anise

2 stalks spring onion, washed, trimmed and halved

6 cloves garlic, peeled and crushed

2 knobs (20 g, 0.7 oz) ginger, peeled and crushed

7 tablespoons good quality dark soy sauce

250 ml (1 cup) water

4 tablespoons raw sugar

2 tablespoons oil

Rinse the duck, both the cavity and outside, with boiling water. This helps remove any odour and impurities. Pat dry with kitchen towels. Rub the duck with the soy sauce and five-spice powder. Set aside for at least 30 minutes.

Heat 2 tablespoons of oil in a wok. Add the cloves, cinnamon, star anise, spring onion, garlic and ginger and fry for 1 minute. Add the dark soy sauce, water and sugar. Bring it up to the boil. Adjust to suit your taste. If the sauce is too salty for you, add a little more water.

Place the duck, breast-side down in the wok, cover, bring the heat to low-medium and cook for 25 minutes, basting the duck once, both inside the cavity and over the duck. Turn the duck over (be careful not to break the skin) and cook covered for a further 25 minutes, basting the duck once, both inside the cavity and over the duck, and again at the end. You may need to turn the duck on either side to ensure the legs and thighs are cooked through and covered with the soy braise. To test if the duck is cooked, run a skewer through the leg joints; if the juices run clear, the duck is cooked.

Remove the duck and allow it to rest for 20-30 minutes before serving. For a thicker gravy, reduce the sauce slightly. Be careful not to over-reduce as it will become too salty. Note that the sauce will also thicken as it cools. Strain through a sieve before serving.

Chop the duck Chinese-style and serve with the gravy and chilli sauce.

NOTE: I use a wok to cook this as its natural curve provides more depth and allows the duck to soak in the sauce. Alternatively, use a deep saucepan that is just a little wider than the duck and adjust the cooking time to cook through.

Keep the extra duck fat for other uses such as Duck Rice. To make Duck Rice, follow the recipe for Chicken Rice (page 25) but with duck fat instead. Also, try roasting your potatoes with rendered duck fat. It's super delicious!

Seafood Sambal

SERVES 4

When I was growing up, my mother often cooked a medley of prawns, fresh squid, fish or fried fresh tofu (tao kwa in Hokkien) in a delicious sambal sauce. This became a dish I could've happily had for dinner everyday! I love prawns, I love fish, and I love squid.... Teamed up with a tangy, hot sambal, you have The Perfect Dish!

200 g (7 oz) squid, cleaned,
   sliced into rings
200 g (7 oz) prawns, peeled, leave
   tail on
200 g (7 oz) white firm fish (ling,
   monkfish, snapper or grouper)
30 g (1 oz) tamarind pulp
1 Spanish onion, peeled, cut into
   wedges
6 tablespoons The Absolute
   Mother of All Sambals
   (page 165)
3 ripe tomatoes, cut into wedges
3 kaffir lime leaves
90 ml extra water
3-4 teaspoons sugar
Pinch of salt
1/4 lemon
3 tablespoons oil

To prepare the tamarind puree, soak the pulp in 120 ml (1/2 cup) warm water until it softens, massage the pulp with your fingers to loosen, then use a sieve and press out as much puree as possible. You should get 6 tablespoons of tamarind liquid.

In a medium saucepan, heat 3 tablespoons of oil over medium heat. Add the onions and stir fry for 1 minute. Add the sambal followed by the tomatoes, kaffir lime leaves, tamarind puree and an additional 90 ml (about 5 tablespoons) of water. Reduce the heat and simmer for 2 minutes or until the tomatoes start to break down slightly. Add the sugar, salt and a squeeze of lemon.

Add the fish and prawns, cook for 1-2 minutes, then finally the squid and cook for another minute until the seafood is just cooked through.

NOTE: Feel free to choose your seafood but add them to the saucepan in the order of how long they take to cook! For example, if you want to add mussels, because they tend to steam open in no time, chuck them in last!

Mom's Fish Curry

SERVES 4

Indian Fish Head Curry is an iconic dish in Singapore and I have eaten my way through many of them. Mom's version has the perfect amount of spices and heat. The fish head has lots of gelatinous bits that really enhances the flavour and texture of the curry. If you are a little reluctant to buy a whole fish head, use cutlets with the bone intact. This recipe uses a whole barramundi.

1 barramundi (800 g, 1.7 lbs), cleaned

1 heaped tablespoon of tamarind pulp

2 medium Japanese eggplants, sliced diagonally

1 large onion, peeled and thickly sliced

2 large red hot chillies, slit down the middle

2 large green chillies, slit down the middle

2 large tomatoes, cut into wedges

12 okra (ladies fingers), stems trimmed, left whole

125 ml ($\frac{1}{2}$ cup) coconut milk

Pinch of sugar

Pinch of salt

SPICE PASTE

1 teaspoon black mustard seeds

1 knob (10 g, 0.35 oz) ginger, peeled and grated

4 cloves garlic, peeled and grated

$\frac{1}{2}$ teaspoon fenugreek seeds

$\frac{1}{2}$ teaspoon fennel seeds, roughly crushed in a mortar and pestle

$1\frac{1}{2}$ teaspoons toasted cumin seeds, roughly crushed in a mortar and pestle

2 stalks curry leaves

2 heaped tablespoons good quality fish curry powder mixed with 2 tablespoons of water to form a wet paste

1 teaspoon chilli powder (optional, add to the curry powder paste)

4 tablespoons oil

To prepare the tamarind liquid, soak the pulp in 355 ml ($1\frac{1}{2}$ cups) warm water until it softens. Massage the pulp with your fingers to loosen and dissolve the tamarind, then sieve to discard the seeds.

In a large saucepan or wok, heat 4 tablespoons of oil over medium-high heat. Add the mustard seeds and fry until they start to pop. Add the rest of the spice paste ingredients and cook for 2-3 minutes until fragrant.

Add the eggplants and fry for 2 minutes, then add the onion and the tamarind liquid and cook for a further 3-4 minutes or until the eggplants are tender. Add the chillies, tomatoes and okra and coconut milk, and season with salt and sugar.

Gently add the fish, ensuring it is mostly submerged in the sauce. Cover and simmer for 4 minutes. Gently turn the fish over and continue to simmer for another couple of minutes until the fish is just cooked.

Serve with steamed rice or roti prata.

NOTE: Freshly-squeezed coconut milk will obviously give the best results. If you are using tinned or carton coconut milk, buy a good brand that has a high percentage of coconut extract.

Soy-Braised Pork Belly with Eggs

SERVES 4

I absolutely love cooking with pork belly. Braising is a great way to render off the fat and what remains is a thin layer of connective tissue that is incredibly tender. If pork belly is really not your thing, use a boneless piece of pork shoulder from a Chinese butcher. This soy braise teams up well with noodles, rice and steamed buns.

750 g (1.6 lbs) pork belly, leave whole or cut into two to fit into the saucepan
4 slices ginger
6 cloves garlic
1 (8 cm, 3 in) cinnamon stick
5 cloves
1 star anise
10 black peppercorns
10 Szechuan peppercorns (optional)
1-2 dried chillies (optional)
5 level tablespoons raw sugar
1 tablespoon Shaoxing wine
2 tablespoons dark soy sauce
250 ml (1 cup) water
6-8 dried shiitake mushrooms, rehydrated in water
4 whole eggs
2 tablespoons oil

Rinse the pork belly with boiling water to remove any impurities.

In a medium saucepan or a pressure cooker, heat 2 tablespoons of oil over medium-high heat. Add the ginger, garlic, spices and dried chilli if using. Fry for 1-2 minutes.

Now put in the pork and sear all around.

Include the sugar and stir until well coated. Deglaze with the Shaoxing wine, then add the soy sauce and water. Stir to combine. Ensure that the skin of the pork is facing up.

Cover with a lid and gently simmer for 1½-2 hours or until tender, turning over halfway through cooking at which time also add the shiitake mushrooms. If the water looks like it's drying up, add a little more water.

If you are using a pressure cooker, cook for 45 minutes at medium pressure. Release the pressure, remove the lid and place on the stove to cook over medium heat for a further 10 minutes until the pork is tender.

Place the eggs in a small-medium pot filled with water. Bring to the boil and cook for about 8-10 minutes. If you prefer a runny yolk, place room temperature eggs in boiling water for exactly 5 minutes. Remove and dunk in cold water to stop the cooking process.

Gently tap the eggs on the table until cracks appear all around the eggs. Place the eggs in the braising liquor to steep for a few hours, or overnight. Make sure that the sauce has cooled down or else the eggs will continue cooking. When ready to serve, peel the eggs for a marbled effect like Tea Eggs.

Slice the pork into 1 cm-thick pieces and pour over the braising liquor. Serve with hot steamed rice or with fresh egg noodles and Asian greens.

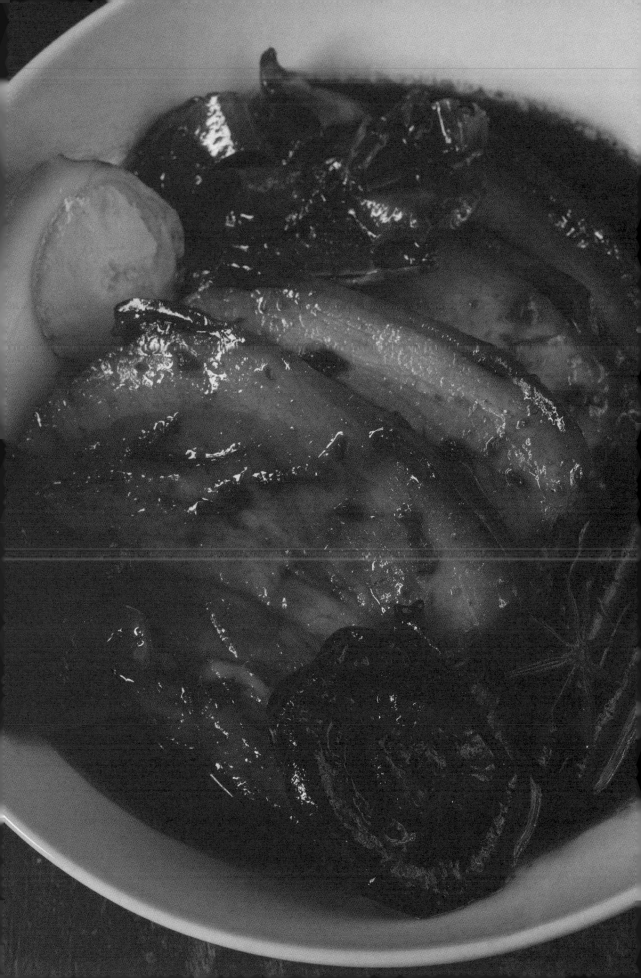

Roast Pork Belly with Szechuan Peppercorns

SERVES 4

If you're in Singapore, you'll be familiar with siu yok or roast pork belly. The alluring bit would be the crackling. There are so many ways to roast pork belly, each offering a slightly different result but equally as good. Cook it correctly and the layers of fat provide incredible amounts of flavour and tenderness as it renders off. Here's a recipe which homes in on the traditional Chinese technique using very simple ingredients.

1 kg pork belly, cleaned
1 teaspoon Szechuan peppercorns
2 teaspoons sea salt
Extra sea salt

Dry roast the peppercorns and 2 teaspoons of sea salt in a dry frying pan over medium heat until fragrant. Remove from the heat, cool and grind the mixture in a mortar and pestle.

Place the pork belly skin-side up and use a sharp metal skewer to poke a million holes all over the skin. Then, using a sharp razor blade or paring knife, score the skin 1 cm (0.4 in) apart.

Generously rub in a handful of sea salt all over the skin. Flip the meat over and rub in the Szechuan pepper and salt mix all over the meat, avoiding the skin.

Place the meat, skin-side up, in the fridge uncovered overnight. This will help draw out excess moisture. For the best results prepare all this a day ahead. The dryer the skin, the crispier the crackling will become in the oven.

Preheat your oven to 220°C (428°F).

Wipe off any excess salt and moisture from the skin. Place a rack over a deep baking tray filled with boiling water. Sit the pork on top of the rack and roast in the oven for 30 minutes. Reduce the temperature to 180°C (356°F) and roast for a further 2 hours, ensuring that the water in the baking tray is topped up as needed. For the final 15-30 minutes, turn on the grill and increase the temperature to 220°C (428°F). You will want to watch this bit like a hawk to avoid burning the pork.

Cover loosely with foil and rest the meat before chopping into bite-sized pieces. Serve with my Fresh Red Chilli Relish (page 169).

NOTE: It's the intense high heat that also creates good pork crackling.

Nasi Lemak

SERVES 4

Nasi Lemak or coconut rice is one of those institutional dishes that everyone loves in Singapore and Malaysia. Back in the 1970s and 1980s, alongside the markets in Johor Bahru, old ladies would sell it wrapped in banana leaf and newspaper. The packets were filled with coconut rice, eggs, a blob of sambal, and deep-fried fish (page 62) or ikan bilis with peanuts (page 62). I could never wait to get home before devouring the contents of the little parcels.

My mother cooks a brilliant Nasi Lemak. Now I cook this quite regularly for my family. There is an art to getting the rice perfect with the right amount of "lemak-ness" or richness. The sambal? Oh my gosh, that and the rice! Happy days!

2 cups long-grain or Jasmine rice, washed until water runs clear, drained
175 ml (¾ cup) water
175 ml (¾ cup) coconut milk
Good pinch of salt
Pandanus leaf, knotted

2-3 tablespoons extra coconut cream, to taste

Put all ingredients except the extra coconut cream into a rice cooker and cook according to the cooker's instructions.

To cook the rice on the stove, put all ingredients except the extra coconut cream in a medium saucepan and bring to the boil over high heat. Stir well, ensuring the rice grains are not stuck to the bottom of the saucepan. Cover with the lid and reduce to the lowest heat possible. Cook for about 10-12 minutes until the rice is cooked through.

To enrich the coconut flavour, add the extra 2-3 tablespoons of coconut cream to the cooked rice. Toss with a fork, cover and leave for 10 minutes.

NOTE: As rice differs depending on the year's crop or the age of the rice, get to know your rice by cooking it a couple of times with your usual ratio of water to rice, then adjust according to your liking. This is my trusted method: After washing the rice clean, I put my index finger on the flattened bed of rice and add enough water to come up to the first joint of the finger. It always works. However, as I like my coconut rice with a little bit of a bite, I use a little less water for Nasi Lemak.

Deep-Fried Fish

SERVES 4

The traditional fish for Nasi Lemak is ikan kuning (yellow-banded scad), but use any small fish you can get at the fish market. If you're not a big fan of eating whole fish on the bone, use a cutlet with bones that are easier to remove.

4 fish (150 g, 5 oz each)
2 teaspoons fish curry powder
½ teaspoon ground turmeric
1 teaspoon chilli powder
1 teaspoon sea salt
Drizzle of oil
2 cloves garlic, peeled and grated
½ knob (5 g, 0.2 oz) ginger,
  peeled and grated
Oil for deep frying

Mix the curry powder, turmeric, chilli powder and sea salt together in a bowl. Rub the spice mix all over the fish. Drizzle over a little oil, cover and refrigerate for a few hours or overnight.

Just before cooking, rub over the grated garlic and ginger.

Heat 80 ml (⅓ cup) of oil in a wok on high heat, or enough oil in your pan to shallow fry. Fry the fishes in batches of 2 for about 2 minutes on each side or until crispy and cooked through. With small fishes, it will take no time at all to cook but you want to get them really nice and crispy.

Serve with Nasi Lemak along with lots of my Absolute Mother of All Sambals (page 165) and Achar (page 168).

Ikan Bilis and Peanuts

SERVES 4

Ikan bilis, or dried anchovies, is available in Asian shops. This classic combo is also a brilliant bar snack since colonial times.

100 g (3.5 oz) ikan bilis (dried
  anchovies)
50 g (1.8 oz) roasted peanuts
1 small Spanish onion, peeled,
  halved, thinly sliced
1 red chilli, thinly sliced on the
  diagonal
1 tablespoon kecap manis
  (Indonesian sweet soy sauce)
Pinch of salt
2-3 tablespoons oil

Preheat your oven to 120°C (248°F).

Rinse the ikan bilis under water. Spread out onto a baking tray and dry in the oven for 20-30 minutes.

Heat 2-3 tablespoons of oil in a frying pan over medium heat and fry the ikan bilis until crispy. Drain on paper towels. Fry the peanuts until lightly golden. Drain on paper towels.

Fry the onions and chilli until soft and slightly blistered. Toss in the ikan bilis and peanuts and drizzle over the sweet soy sauce and add the salt. Toss well. Cool and store in an airtight jar until ready to use.

Dry-Style Assam Prawns

SERVES 4

Tamarind, or assam as it is called in Singapore, Malaysia and Indonesia, is one of my pantry staples. I use tamarind pulp because it stores well and you can control how concentrated you'd like the tamarind liquid to be. It's probably what lemon juice is to western cooking but it is far more sophisticated in flavour. The sourness works so well with a whole host of dishes. This is a really simple, rustic and delicious dish, and one that Mom used to cook often for me, "The Prawn Queen". It makes a luxurious accompaniment for Nasi Lemak.

500 g (1.1 lbs) king prawns, whiskers trimmed, deveined leaving shells intact
2 tablespoons tamarind pulp
1 teaspoon sea salt
Pinch of sugar
2 cloves garlic, peeled and finely chopped
2 tablespoons oil

To prepare the tamarind puree, soak the pulp in 240 ml (1 cup) warm water until it softens, massage the pulp with your fingers to loosen, then use a sieve and press out as much puree as possible.

Marinade the prawns with the tamarind puree, salt and sugar for 30 minutes.

Heat 2 tablespoons of oil in a wok or frying pan over high heat. Add the garlic and fry briefly. Drain the prawns and add to the wok. Stir fry until just cooked.

Serve immediately.

Hokkien Noodles with Mushrooms and Wood Ear Fungus

SERVES 4

Noodles are an important part of Chinese cuisine and culture. They are always served during Chinese New Year or birthday celebrations. The long strands of noodles are left intact as they represent long life. Hokkien noodles – yellow egg noodles – are a staple in my household as they are quick to cook and come in handy during the busy week.

I love the simplicity of cooking a wholly vegetarian dish with lots of mushrooms and greens, but feel free to add some chicken, beef, pork or prawns if you like. If you are cooking Hokkien noodles with soup, blanch the noodles in boiling water and drain before using. But if you're frying up a wok of noodles, then it comes straight out of the pack and into the wok!

500 g (1.1 lbs) Hokkien noodles (yellow egg noodles)

3 cloves garlic, peeled, finely chopped

1 knob (10 g, 0.35 oz) ginger, peeled, finely chopped

100 g (3.5 oz) wood ear fungus, torn into bite-sized pieces

100 g (3.5 oz) fresh shiitake mushroom, sliced or halved

1 bunch of choy sum (mustard greens), trimmed and cut into 5 cm (2 in) lengths

100 g (3.5 oz) oyster mushroom, torn into bite-sized pieces

100 g (3.5 oz) shimeji mushroom, break into bite-sized pieces

2 tablespoons oyster sauce

2 tablespoons Shaoxing wine

1 tablespoon light soy sauce

1 teaspoon ground white pepper

1 teaspoon sesame oil

2 stalks spring onion, trimmed and cut into 5 cm (2 in) lengths

3 tablespoons oil

Crispy shallots

Pickled Green Chillies (page 167)

Heat 3 tablespoons of oil in a large pot or wok over medium-high heat. Fry the garlic and ginger for 1 minute. Add the wood ear fungus, shiitake and choy sum and fry for a further 2 minutes or until the greens have wilted slightly. Add the other mushrooms and toss, then put in the oyster sauce, Shaoxing wine, light soy sauce, pepper and sesame oil.

Include the noodles and spring onions and toss to combine. Taste and adjust seasoning to your taste.

Top with crispy shallots and my Pickled Green Chillies (page 167) and serve immediately.

On the Grill

Cooking on the grill, whether it's over the barbecue or on a griddle pan, creates lovely flavours, particularly when the food is a tad charred. You often hear chefs using the word caramelisation and it is this that creates depth of flavour.

Living in Sydney over the past decade has given me an added appreciation of cooking food differently. Whilst much of my cooking is done over the stove, I never decline an opportunity to cook over an open flame. I've moved from using a gas barbecue for its convenience to now preferring to cook over coals.

My trip to Cambodia taught me much about cooking over an open flame and knowing how to manage the heat. Cooking has never been more exciting!

Spiced Butterflied Chicken

SERVES 4

I love cooking chicken, and cooking it on the bone makes it just that much more flavoursome. Apart from a roast chook, we often choose to cook with boneless fillets for mere ease and convenience. But I encourage you to get back to the "bone" basics and you will not be disappointed. This recipe is inspired by my Indian-Singaporean heritage and uses a combination of Indian spices, both dry and wet. Cook it on the bar-b!

1 large free-range chicken, cleaned, excess fat removed from the cavity
½ teaspoon smoked salt or sea salt
1 tablespoon olive oil
¼ lemon

MARINADE
1 teaspoon cumin seeds, toasted and ground
1 teaspoon coriander seeds, toasted and ground
5 green cardamom pods, toasted and ground
3 whole cloves, toasted and ground
1 knob (10 g, 0.35 oz) ginger, grated
4 cloves garlic, skinned and grated
1 large red chilli, finely chopped
1 knob (10 g, 0.35 oz) fresh turmeric, finely chopped
1 sprig coriander, including root and stems, washed and finely chopped
Good pinch of sugar
¼ lemon, zest and juice
1 tablespoon vegetable oil
2 teaspoons smoked sea salt or to taste

YOGHURT MIX
120 ml (½ cup) yoghurt
1 tablespoon honey
2 tablespoons almond meal or coarsely chopped almonds

Prepare the marinade by toasting all the dry spices and grinding them in a mortar and pestle, then mixing everything together to form a marinade.

Prepare the yoghurt mix by mixing all the ingredients.

Place the chicken on a chopping board, breast-side down. Using a sharp knife, score down the middle of the back bone from the neck down to the tail. Then, using a pair of sharp kitchen scissors, follow the knife score and cut through the bone. Flatten out the chicken. The chicken breasts should now be in the middle and facing upwards. Cover with cling film and use a meat mallet or rolling pin and gently, but firmly, thump it until it flattens evenly, or flatten the bird firmly with the palms of your hands.

Gently separate the skin of the chicken from the flesh starting from the breast, then feed the marinade gently under the skin into the flesh, pushing it down into the legs.

Spoon the combined yoghurt mix under the skin and ensure it flows through to the legs and thighs.

Rub the outside of the chicken with a little salt, olive oil and lemon juice.

Line a baking tray with two layers of foil ensuring that the edges are folded up to catch any excess juices. Bake in an oven preheated to 200°C (392°F) for 50 minutes to 1 hour, then reduce to 150°C (302°F) for a further half hour. For a smaller chicken, bake at 180°C (356°F) for 45 minutes to 1 hour. If you are baking in a barbecue, bake at low heat for about an hour. To test if the chicken is cooked, pierce the joints near the legs and juices should run clear. Rest the chicken for 10-15 minutes before serving.

Reserve the juices from the cooking and pour over the chicken when serving.

Serve with some shredded purple cabbage or roasted pumpkin and spinach leaves, chillies and a light vinaigrette. See the section on salads from page 139 for ideas.

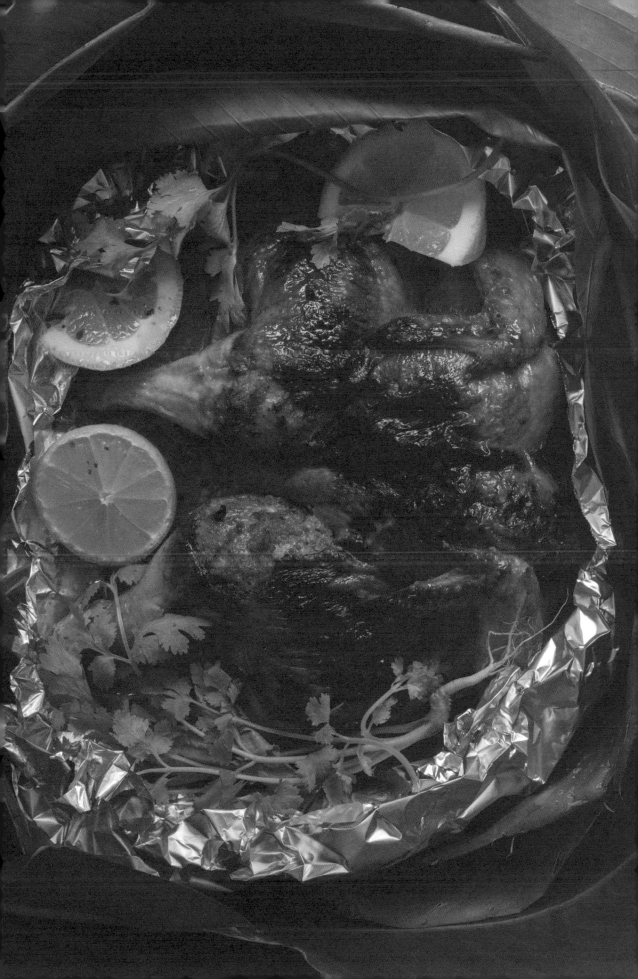

Grilled Squid with Spiced Prawn Stuffing

SERVES 4

Squid or sotong in Malay is quick and simple to cook. Mom used to cook stuffed sambal squid when I was a child and those memories are still vibrantly alive in my mind. I'm taking everything I love about Southeast Asian ingredients and cooking it on the barbecue!

4 squids (85 g, 3 oz each),
    cleaned, tentacles separated
    and kept for stuffing
Pinch of salt
2 tablespoons oil
1 cup coconut cream
1 teaspoon sugar
Dash of fish sauce

STUFFING
200 g (7 oz) prawn meat, roughly
    chopped
2 cloves garlic, peeled, finely
    chopped
1 knob (10 g. 0.35 oz) ginger,
    peeled, finely chopped
½ long hot red chilli, finely
    chopped
1 heaped teaspoon red curry
    paste
Pinch of salt
Pinch of sugar
1 large kaffir lime leaf, finely
    chopped
2 teaspoons chopped coriander
    stems and leaves

Chop finely the tentacles of the squid.

To make the stuffing, heat 2 tablespoons of oil in a saucepan over medium heat. Add the garlic, ginger and chilli and fry for 30 seconds. Add the curry paste, prawns and chopped tentacles. Stir to break up any lumps. Season with salt and sugar then add the kaffir lime leaves and coriander. Toss and set aside to cool.

Stuff the squid loosely and use a toothpick to secure the ends. Score the squid lightly, drizzle with oil and season with a pinch of salt.

Over a hot grill or barbecue, cook the squid for about a minute or two over high heat on each side until golden and lightly charred. Squid doesn't take long at all to cook, so watch closely.

While the grilled squid is resting, heat the coconut cream, sugar and fish sauce in a small saucepan over medium heat. Stir until the sugar has dissolved.

Slice the squid up on the diagonal into 4-5 pieces then pour over the coconut cream sauce. Serve immediately.

NOTE: If you like to omit the coconut cream, simply drizzle the cooked squid with kecap manis (Indonesian sweet soy sauce). It'll be just as good!

BBQ King Prawns

SERVES 4

12 large tiger king prawns
  (500 g, 1.1 lbs), whiskers and
  legs trimmed, deveined,
  butterflied

MARINADE
3 cloves garlic, peeled and
  coarsely grated
1 long red chilli, finely chopped
1 small bunch fresh coriander,
  washed, trimmed, finely
  chopped
1 lemon, zest
Squeeze of lemon juice
Pinch of sugar
Pinch of smoked salt or sea salt
3 tablespoons olive oil

In a bowl, mix all the marinade ingredients together. Pour the marinade over the prawns. Mix well. Refrigerate for 20 minutes.

Barbecue the prawns shell-side down for 2-3 minutes, then turn over briefly until just cooked.

Squeeze over a little more lemon juice and serve immediately.

Grilled Sambal Sea Perch

SERVES 4-6

Summertime calls for more outdoor cooking in Sydney. With great, warm weather, cooking food on the barbecue brings a different focus to the meal. We often end up eating outdoors and mealtimes become fun and social affairs. I take these opportunities to cook fish and fish grilled on the barbecue over coals is insanely flavoursome. This really simple dish using my Laksa spice paste (page 160) is one which you will cook over and over again.

2 deep sea perch (650 g, 1.4 lbs
  each), scaled, cleaned and
  butterflied

MARINADE
2 tablespoons laksa spice paste
  (page 160)
2 teaspoons coconut milk powder
1 teaspoon brown sugar
$\frac{1}{2}$ teaspoon sea salt
4 tablespoons oil
Squeeze of lime juice

If you'd like to try butterflying your own fish, here's how you do it. Use scissors to cut off both gills. Run your filleting knife from the tail along the spine to the head, then tease your way alongside the bone to as close as possible to the belly but don't cut right through the fish. Open up and flatten firmly with the palms of your hands.

You can go further and debone the fish by doing the same thing on the other side of the spine. Clip away the spine.

Mix the marinade together in a bowl. Baste both sides of the fish and grill for 4-5 minutes on the flesh side, then turn over and grill for a couple more minutes or until the fish is cooked through and lightly charred. Squeeze over a little lemon juice and serve immediately.

Sticky Orange Marmalade Pork Ribs

SERVES 4

Sweet, salty, sticky tender pork ribs — make them like this and you'll have the neighbours lining up at your door! These are always a hit when I make them at home. Forget knives and forks and just tuck in with your fingers!

1.6 kg (3.5 lbs) American pork ribs, leave whole
1 tablespoon coriander seeds, dry roasted, ground

MARINADE
4 cloves garlic, grated
2 oranges, zest and juice
4 tablespoons good quality marmalade
3 tablespoons dark brown sugar
2 teaspoons smoked salt or sea salt
1 teaspoon chilli flakes
2 tablespoons red wine or malt vinegar
2 tablespoons olive oil

Rub the coriander seeds over the pork.

Mix all the other ingredients together in a bowl. Place the pork ribs in a large baking pan and pour over the marinade, massaging it into the pork. Cover and leave to marinate for at least an hour or overnight in the fridge.

Remove from the fridge 10 minutes before baking. Preheat your oven to 180°C (356°F). Cover with foil and bake for 1 hour. Remove the foil and bake for a further hour or until the ribs are tender and sticky, basting once or twice as the sauce thickens. If the marinade looks a little dry in the pan before this time, pour in about 60 ml (¼ cup) of water to prevent the marinade from burning.

Smoked Salt, Avocado Oil Angus Rump

SERVES 4

One of the joys of living in Australia is the abundant, fabulous produce. I've been blessed to have had the opportunity to cook with some of the most amazing meats produced locally. Use the best quality meat, cook it well and you will get the most beautifully tender result. This is a big favourite at my private-dining events.

800 g (1.7 lbs) Australian Angus Rump, 5 cm (2 in) thick
1½-2 teaspoons smoked salt
2-3 tablespoons avocado oil or extra virgin olive oil

Preheat your oven to 180°C (356°F).

Marinate the beef by rubbing on a sprinkling of smoked sea salt and a good drizzle of avocado oil or extra virgin olive oil. Set aside for at least 10 minutes.

Heat an ovenproof griddle or frying pan on high heat, and sear the rump on both sides until nicely caramelised and charred. Place in the oven and cook for 10 minutes or until medium rare. The internal temperature of the meat should be approximately 55°C (131°F).

If your cut of beef is thinner, you may choose to cook the beef solely over the stove, ensuring that the meat is cooked to medium-rare.

Alternatively, you will get great results from cooking your beef over the barbecue grill.

Remove from the oven, place on a plate, cover loosely with foil and leave to rest for 10 minutes.

Slice thinly on the diagonal and across the grain, and serve with my Herb Salad (page 140) or Raw Mushroom Salad (page 154).

NOTE: The Original Smoke & Spice Co produces an incredible product: sea salt smoked over manuka wood and tumbled with dried chillies, garlic flakes, herbs and spices. The garlic-infused avocado oil made by Grove is a wonderful product that is perfect for this dish.

My Asian Classics

These dishes range from the simplicity of deep-fried tofu and raw salmon to curries and rich braises using one of my favourite cut of beef, the marbly-ribs. Whether they are old, traditional favourites or newly-inspired dishes using the wonderful produce in Australia, they all have one thing in common – they are scrumptious and everyone loves them!

These dishes feature on my catering menu quite often and they all bring great joy to the dinner table.

Chicken Sang Choy Bao with Green Curry Paste

SERVES 4

Everyone must have had Sang Choy Bao at least once in their life at a Chinese restaurant. I love the concept of the way it's eaten. In this recipe, the flavours of freshly-made green curry paste takes it to another level. Please do try and make your own green curry paste. It's so much fresher in flavours and vibrantly green than store-bought paste!

500 g (1.1 lbs) minced chicken
8 iceberg lettuce or 16 baby
   cos lettuce cups, washed and
   drained well
2 tablespoons fish sauce
1-2 tablespoons gula melaka
   (coconut sugar) or brown sugar
3 cloves garlic, finely minced
2 teaspoons ginger, finely grated
1 tablespoon green curry paste
   (page 163)
2 large kaffir lime leaves, finely
   julienned
2 red chillies, thinly sliced
   (deseeded if preferred)
1 level tablespoon tapioca flour
   or cornflour, mixed with
   1 tablespoon water to form a
   slurry (optional)
3 stalks spring onions, thinly
   sliced
2 sprigs coriander or to your
   liking, chopped
Squeeze of lime juice
1 cucumber, finely sliced
3 tablespoons toasted peanuts,
   coarsely ground
2 tablespoons crispy shallots
2 tablespoons oil

In a small glass bowl, mix together the fish sauce and sugar. Set aside.

Heat 2 tablespoons of oil in a wok or frying pan over medium-high heat, add the garlic and ginger and fry for 1 minute.

Add the minced chicken, cook for 3 to 4 minutes until slightly coloured or until just cooked, using your spatula to break up any lumps.

Add the green curry paste, the fish sauce and sugar mixture, kaffir lime leaves and red chillies. Cook for 2-3 minutes, mixing well. Adjust seasoning to taste with more fish sauce if you wish.

If using the tapioca flour or cornflour slurry to thicken, pour over now and mix well. Cook a further 1 minute. Mix in the spring onions and fresh coriander and toss for a minute. Remove from the heat and add the lime juice. Mix well.

Fill each lettuce cup with the filling, top with cucumber, peanuts and crispy shallots. Serve immediately.

NOTE: Green curry paste can be purchased from any Asian grocery store. However, try making your own and taste the freshness of the real thing.

The tapioca flour or cornflour can be mixed through the chicken before frying. This will help keep the chicken mince moist.

The amount of toppings and fresh herbs may be adjusted to your taste.

Dong Po Pork

SERVES 2-4

The Chinese have created a million and one dishes using pork belly and one of their favourite ways to eat it is to cook it until the fat literally melts in your mouth. Dong Po Pork, using this technique, is cooked in a very light braising marinade. I often cook this using my pressure cooker to halve the time. To maintain the shape of the pork, I sometimes tie it with butcher's twine.

500 g (1.1 lbs) pork belly
1 knob (10 g, 0.35 oz) ginger, peeled and sliced thickly
3 stalks spring onion, washed, cut into 6 cm (about 2.5 in) lengths
2 tablespoon dark soy sauce
1 tablespoon light soy sauce
3 tablespoons Shaoxing wine
40 g (1.4 oz) rock sugar or 2 tablespoons brown sugar
1 tablespoon oil

Heat 1 tablespoon of oil in a medium-sized saucepan over high heat. Put in the pork belly, skin-side down, and fry until the skin is slightly blistered, about 5 minutes. Remove the pork and set aside. Keep 1 tablespoon of oil and remove the rest as there will be a lot more oil from rendering the skin.

Fry the ginger and spring onions for a minute or two in the same saucepan until fragrant. Add all the other ingredients along with 250 ml (1 cup) of water and bring to the boil. Return the pork to the saucepan skin-side down and simmer covered for 30 minutes. Carefully turn the pork over and simmer for a further 2 hours or until it is very tender.

If baking in the oven, preheat the oven to 180°C (356°F). Render the pork in a pan on the stove as above. Place all the ingredients in a medium ovenproof dish, with the pork skin-side down. Cover with foil and bake for 30 minutes. Carefully turn the pork over, cover with foil again and return to the oven for a further 2 hours until the pork is very tender. If you prefer the skin to be crispy, increase the oven temperature to 200°C (392°F), remove the foil and place under the grill. Cook until the skin crackles to your liking. Be careful not to burn the skin.

Remove the pork and set aside to rest. Place the braising liquid over the stove and reduce slightly. Adjust seasoning to your taste with extra sugar or dark soy.

Remove the butcher's twine if using. Serve the pork and sauce with steamed rice and some stir-fried Asian greens.

Sticky Tamarind Prawns

SERVES 2-4

I have had the pleasure to work with Singapore Tourism Board on a number of campaigns to promote Singapore as the place to visit. On a recent gig, I created this dish – full of vibrant colours, familiar flavours, traditions and a touch of modernity – to represent My Singapore. The sticky, tangy, sweet and salty prawns make an insanely delicious dish that every Singaporean and visitor to my hometown will love to tuck into.

350 g (12.5 oz) black tiger king prawns, about 8 medium prawns

1 teaspoon coarsely ground white pepper

¾ teaspoon smoked salt or sea salt

50 g (1.8 oz) tamarind pulp

200 ml (0.8 cup) warm water

2-3 cups oil

2 cloves garlic, peeled and sliced

1 large red chilli, sliced, remove seeds to reduce heat

50 g (1.8 oz) gula melaka (coconut sugar) or dark brown sugar

½ lime

¼ cup coriander leaves

¼ cup mint leaves

½ stalk spring onion, sliced thinly on the diagonal

Edible flowers for garnishing (optional)

Prepare the prawns by trimming the whiskers, removing the shells but leaving the heads and tail intact. Butterfly the prawns by running a knife down the back, devein. Place in a bowl and marinate well with the white pepper and smoked salt. Set aside.

To prepare the tamarind puree, soak the pulp in 240 ml (1 cup) warm water until it softens, massage the pulp with your fingers to loosen, then use a sieve and press out as much puree as possible.

Preheat 2-3 cups of oil in a wok or saucepan until 180°C (356°F). Gently lower each prawn into the hot oil and fry for a couple of minutes until the prawns are just cooked through. Remove and drain on some kitchen towels.

Remove all but 2 tablespoons of oil from the wok and heat over high heat. Add the garlic and chilli and fry until lightly golden. Add the gula melaka and tamarind puree and cook until smooth and thick, about 1-2 minutes. Return the prawns to the wok, add a squeeze of lime juice and toss until well coated. Remove from the heat.

To plate, toss the herbs together in a bowl with a squeeze of lime juice and transfer onto a serving plate. Place the prawns over the herbs, and decorate with the sliced spring onion and edible flowers. Serve immediately with steamed rice.

Crispy Fried Tofu with Szechuan Pepper

SERVES 4-6

The simplest of dishes is sometimes the most delicious! Tofu is one of the ingredients I really love to cook with. There are a myriad of varieties to choose from: Fresh tofu, tau kwa (the deep-fried variety) to silken tofu and so on. Since they don't contain much flavour in themselves, what you add to tofu creates the dish. So be inventive and give it a go!

800 g (1.7 lbs) fresh tofu, cut into large cubes
1 teaspoon Szechuan peppercorn
2 teaspoons sea salt
¼ cup rice flour
Vegetable oil for deep frying

Drain the tofu between some kitchen towels to extract any excess water. Pat dry.

In a deep-fryer or small-medium saucepan, heat the vegetable oil until it reaches about 180°C (356°F). A good way to test if the oil is hot enough is to place a wooden chopstick wiped with a damp cloth in the oil, and if it sizzles and starts bubbling around the chopstick, the oil is ready.

In the meantime, dry roast the Szechuan peppercorn and salt over medium heat in a frying pan until fragrant. This will take about 2-3 minutes. Cool and grind to a powder using a mortar and pestle.

Mix a teaspoon of Szechuan salt with the rice flour, and keep the remaining Szechuan salt aside. Coat the tofu in this mix and deep fry until lightly golden. Drain on paper towels.

Sprinkle on a pinch of the reserved Szechuan salt and serve immediately.

Crispy-Skin Chicken with Dark Soy and Black Vinegar Dressing

SERVES 4-6

I've got to admit that I'm not a huge fan of chicken skin. BUT, this is one of the dishes where the chicken skin is somewhat divine, nicely salted and crispy! I've been able to play with a variety of methods to crisp up skin. The secret is in drying out the skin prior to deep frying – the drier, the crispier! Poaching the chicken beforehand keeps it incredibly delicious and succulent! This dish is inspired by a Kylie Kwong recipe.

1 whole chicken (1.8 kg, 4 lbs), cleaned, excess fat from cavity removed
2 stalks spring onion, trimmed, cut into 4 each
6 cloves garlic, crushed
1 large knob (20 g, 0.7 oz) ginger, bruised
Oil for deep frying

DRESSING
1 tablespoon dark soy sauce
2 tablespoons black vinegar
1 tablespoon light soy sauce
1 tablespoon poaching stock
1 teaspoon sesame oil
1 teaspoon chilli oil
2 teaspoons raw sugar
$\frac{1}{4}$ teaspoon freshly ground Szechuan pepper
1 red chilli, finely chopped
2 sprigs coriander stems and roots, finely sliced
2 stalks spring onion, finely sliced

Fill a pot a little larger than the chicken with just enough water to cover the chicken. Add the spring onions, garlic and ginger and bring to the boil. Gently lower the chicken into the pot, bring it back to the boil, then immediately lower the heat so that the water barely bubbles. Cover and cook for 20 minutes. Turn the heat off and let the chicken cool in the stock, about 3 hours. This is White Poached Chicken.

Remove the chicken from the pot. Place in the refrigerator uncovered for a few hours or overnight to dry out the skin.

Prepare the Dark Soy and Black Vinegar Dressing by mixing all the dressing ingredients.

Preheat about 3 to 4 cups of oil in a wok or deep-fryer to 180°C (356°F). Remove the chicken from the fridge at least half an hour beforehand. This will allow the chicken to come to room temperature. Halve the chicken right down the breastbone through to the back. Pat dry and deep fry each half until crispy and golden. Chop the chicken Chinese style, top with lots of shredded spring onions and pour over a few tablespoons of the dressing just before serving.

You can also serve the White Poached Chicken with my Fresh Red Chilli Relish (page 167), Ginger and Shallot Relish (page 169) and Chicken Rice (page 25). Just mix a teaspoon of light soy with a teaspoon of sesame oil and brush over the chicken skin prior to chopping.

NOTE: Cooking the chicken over gentle heat and leaving it to cool in the stock creates a succulent, moist result. When deep frying the chicken, be careful as the juicy meat might cause the oil to spit.

If you do not wish to deep fry the chicken, then roast at 180°C (356°F), turning the temperature up to 200°C (392°F) in the final stages to get the skin crispy.

Chilli Pepper Roast Duck

SERVES 4

If duck is your thing, then you'll definitely have to try this recipe. Master a few tips and techniques and the rest is incredibly easy. Make sure you start with a beautifully plump and fresh duck. The trick to a crispy-skin duck is to keep the skin dry before roasting!

1 duck (2 kg, 4.4 lbs), cleaned, cavity fat and neck removed, pat dry
1 knob (10 g, 0.35 oz) ginger, sliced
4 cloves garlic, crushed
10 g (0.35 oz) fresh mandarin peel
1 teaspoon mandarin juice
1 teaspoon oil

SPICE RUB
1 teaspoon Szechuan peppercorn
½ teaspoon white peppercorns
½ teaspoon chilli flakes
¾ teaspoon sea salt

If possible, prepare the duck a day ahead or a few hours before cooking.

In a dry frying pan, roast the Szechuan peppercorns, white peppercorns, chilli flakes and salt until fragrant. Remove from heat and cool. Grind to a coarse powder in a mortar and pestle. Set aside in a small bowl.

Using a sharp metal skewer or a small pointed knife, prick holes all over the fatty part of the duck (breast, neck, cavity opening). Rub the duck with the mandarin juice then rub the spice rub all over the duck, including inside the cavity. Place the garlic, ginger and mandarin peel in the cavity of the duck. Drizzle and rub the oil all over the duck.

Air dry the duck in the fridge uncovered until ready to cook. This helps to dry the skin for a crispier finish.

Preheat the oven to 180°C (356°F).

Place the duck breast-side up on a rack over a baking tray lined with foil. This will help to catch all the drippings. Roast for 1 hour 45 minutes. Increase the temperature to 200°C (392°F) and roast for a further 15 minutes. The average cooking time for duck is 45 minutes per kilogram. However, I find that a little bit of extra cooking time at high heat crispens the skin a touch more.

Remove from the oven, cover loosely with foil and rest for 20 minutes before serving. You should be able to pull the duck apart with your hands!

This duck is great with my Fresh Red Chilli Relish (page 167).

NOTE: The duck fat and drippings can be kept and used to make Duck Rice. To make Duck Rice, use the recipe for Chicken Rice (page 25) but with duck fat instead.

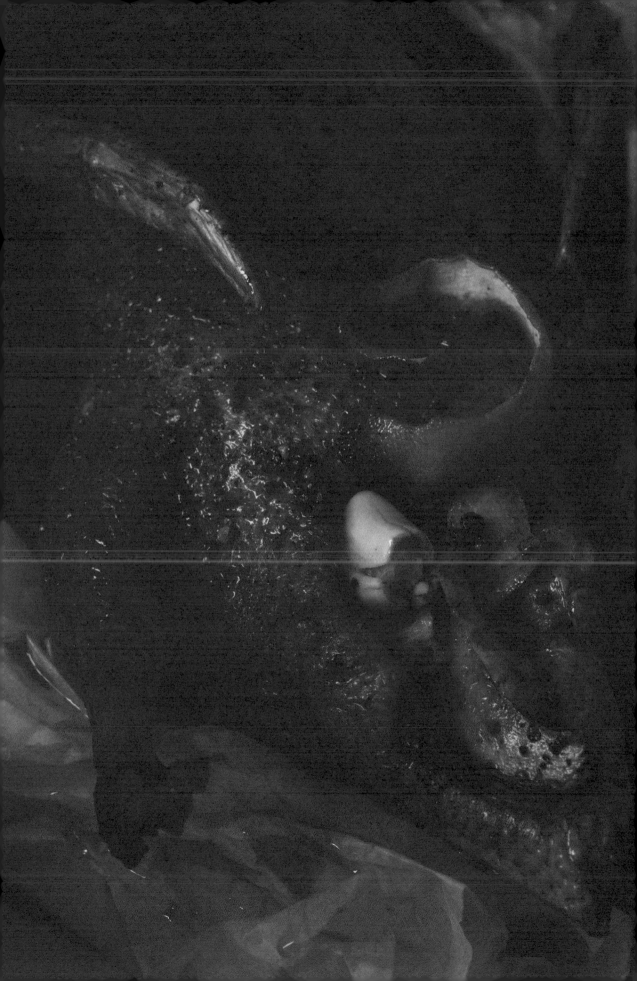

Ayam Masak Merah
(Malay Spicy Chicken)

SERVES 4-6

This is a really popular Malay dish and there are countless versions. This is my mom's version, a slightly modern take using tomato ketchup! She cooks it with huge chicken wings and it's absolutely finger lickin' delicious. I used to scrape up the sauce – full of blistered onions and chillies and peas – and simply ate it with hot steamed rice. Unbelievably good!

1 (1½ kg, 3.3 lbs) whole
   chicken, cut into 14 pieces
4 large tomatoes, quartered
8 tablespoons tomato ketchup
4 teaspoons sugar
2 tablespoons lemon juice
¼ cup green peas, frozen or fresh
Oil

MARINADE
2 large red chillies, slit into half
   lengthways
2 cloves garlic, crushed, skin
   removed
15 g (5 oz) ginger, peeled and
   bruised
1 teaspoon salt
1 teaspoon sugar
1 teaspoon white pepper
1 large Spanish onion, peeled
   and quartered

Mix the marinade ingredients then add the chicken and mix well. Marinate for a few hours or overnight in the fridge.

Preheat the oil for deep frying. Fry the chicken pieces for 5-7 minutes until golden and almost cooked. Remove and set aside.

In a wok or saucepan, heat 1 tablespoon of oil over medium-high heat. Fry the marinade of chillies, garlic, ginger and onions for 2 minutes until slightly softened and blistered.

Add the fresh tomatoes, ketchup, sugar, lemon juice, 4 tablespoons of water and cook for another minute.

Put the chicken into the sauce and stir well. Add the peas, reduce the heat to low, cover and simmer for about 15 minutes until the chicken is cooked through and the sauce has thickened.

Beef Rendang

SERVES 4

This is a classic dish. What makes a rendang is the addition of kerisik (toasted grated coconut). It gives it big flavours and richness! There are so many different versions of rendang stretching across Indonesia, Malaysia and even within Singapore. You'll find that everyone cooks it differently.

My mother's version is much simpler in flavours but delicious nonetheless. This is my version, rich and robust and leaves you salivating and wanting more!

1 kg (2.2 lbs) chuck steak, excess
   fat trimmed, cut into 6 cm
   (2.5 in) cubes
2 tablespoons ground coriander
1 teaspoon ground cumin
½ teaspoon ground fennel
1 teaspoon sweet paprika
375 ml (1½ cups) coconut milk
3-4 heaped tablespoons fresh
   grated coconut or desiccated
   coconut
2 teaspoons salt or to taste
2-3 teaspoons sugar
Oil

SPICE PASTE
20 large dried red chillies,
   soaked or scalded in hot water
   until slightly softened, drained
2 long fresh hot red chillies,
   roughly chopped
15 g (5 oz) galangal, roughly
   chopped
15 g (5 oz) ginger, roughly
   chopped
1 knob (10 g, 0.35 oz) turmeric,
   roughly chopped or
   1 teaspoon ground turmeric
2 stalks lemongrass, white
   to light green part, roughly
   chopped
4 cloves garlic, skin removed
2 medium Spanish onions,
   peeled, roughly chopped

In a food processor or mortar and pestle, grind the dried chillies, fresh chillies, galangal, ginger, turmeric, lemongrass, garlic and onion to a paste.

Heat ¼ cup of oil in a large saucepan over medium heat, add the spice paste and fry until fragrant, stirring frequently. This will take about 8-10 minutes.

Add the coriander, cumin, fennel and paprika and cook for a further 2 minutes. Increase the heat to high and add the beef, stirring until all the beef has been coated with the spice paste.

Add the coconut milk and bring to the boil. Give it a good stir, then lower the heat to low-medium. Cover, leaving a little gap, and cook for 1½ hours, stirring once or twice to avoid anything catching at the bottom of the pan.

While the meat is stewing, fry the grated coconut in a dry pan over medium heat, tossing continuously until dark golden. Remove and set aside.

Add the toasted coconut (kerisik), along with the salt and sugar to the beef and mix well. Cook for a further 15 minutes.

NOTE: Rendang, like most curries can be cooked a day or two ahead of serving. In fact, this allows the flavours to really develop. I like using chuck steak to cook rendang. This cut contains connective tissue that results in a very tender finish after long and slow cooking.

Red Curry Snapper in Banana Leaf (Fish Amok)
SERVES 4

The use of banana leaves in Asian cooking is for two purposes: To act as a plate as well as to flavour the food cooked within it. The natural oils are immediately drawn out when heat is applied; food just tastes that much better as a result. This is a really simple and rather light dish which I picked up while travelling in Cambodia. It's one of the millions of versions of Cambodia's famous Fish Amok.

400 g (14 oz) skinless tender white fish fillets (snapper or monkfish)
4 teaspoons red curry paste (page 162)
120 ml (½ cup) coconut cream
2½ teaspoons fish sauce
1 teaspoon sugar
1 tablespoon vegetable stock
1 large kaffir lime leaf, finely julienned
2-3 thinly sliced lemons, finely wedged
1 red chilli, thinly sliced
1 sprig coriander leaf, picked for garnishing
Banana leaves to make 8 banana leaf cups

Fill a steamer pot with water, remove the steaming racks and bring to the boil.

Mix 4 teaspoons red curry paste with the coconut cream, fish sauce, sugar and stock.

Slice the fish into strips ½ cm (0.2 in) thick. Cut the banana leaves into 15 cm diameter discs. Fold each disc and secure with staples or toothpicks to create a shallow cup. Fill each cup with equal number of fish strips, then add 2 -3 tablespoons of red curry coconut sauce. Top with finely julienne kaffir lime leaves, thin lemon slices, red chillies and coriander leaves. Steam for 10-12 minutes or until the fish is just cooked.

Serve hot with steamed rice.

Green Curry with King Prawns
SERVES 4

1 kg (2.2 lbs) king prawns, peeled, cleaned, tails left intact and butterflied
2 tablespoons green curry paste (page 163)
4 tablespoons oil
300 ml (1.2 cups) coconut cream
1 tablespoon fish sauce
½ tablespoon grated palm sugar
150 ml (0.6 cup) water
2 kaffir lime leaves
½ lime

Fry the green curry paste in the oil over medium heat until fragrant. Add the coconut cream and cook until the oil starts to separate. This will take about 3-4 minutes.

Add the fish sauce and grated palm sugar along with the water. Stir until well dissolved. Crush in the kaffir lime leaves and toss in the king prawns.

Poach until the prawns are just cooked. If you like more sauce, add another couple of tablespoons of water. Squeeze in the juice of the lime, taste and adjust with more palm sugar and fish sauce to your liking. Serve with steamed Jasmine rice.

Tamarind Beef Ribs

SERVES 4

My mouth waters just thinking about this dish. It is traditionally cooked with pork (Babi Assam) but beef ribs work incredibly well. If you can't find beef ribs, then, by all means, use either pork belly or pork spare ribs cut into large chunks. I absolutely love the treacly sweetness of the gula melaka with the tartness of the tamarind. Add to that chillies, kaffir lime leaves and lemongrass, and you have one of the best Nonya dishes! This is what sweet and sour is all about!

1 kg (2.2 lbs) beef ribs, cleaned, excess fat trimmed, cut into large pieces

¾ tablespoon tamarind pulp

1 large Spanish onion, peeled and cut into wedges

2 large hot red chillies, slit into half lengthwise

2 large hot green chillies, slit into half lengthwise

4 cloves garlic, peeled and crushed

1½ tablespoons preserved soy bean paste (tao cheo), slightly mushed

2-3 stalks lemongrass, white part only, bruised

1½ tablespoons dark soy sauce

2 tablespoons gula melaka (coconut sugar) or dark brown sugar

2 large ripe tomatoes, wedged

4 large kaffir lime leaves

Oil

To prepare the tamarind puree, soak the pulp in 240 ml (1 cup) warm water until it softens, massage the pulp with your fingers to loosen, then use a sieve and press out as much puree as possible.

Heat 2 tablespoons of oil in a medium-sized saucepan over medium-high heat. Fry the meat to seal and render off some of the fat. Remove and set aside.

Remove all but 1 tablespoon of oil from the saucepan. Add the onion and chillies and fry until lightly blistered. Remove and set aside.

Fry the garlic, preserved soy bean paste and lemongrass in the same saucepan until fragrant.

Put the meat back into the saucepan and continue frying for a further 1 minute. Add the dark soy sauce, then the gula melaka and toss well.

Include the tamarind puree and bring to the boil.

Lower the heat and simmer covered until the meat is tender and the gravy is rich and thick, about 1½-2 hours. You may need to top up with a little water if the gravy dries up. This part of the cooking can be done in a pressure cooker. Cook on medium pressure for about 45 minutes.

To finish off the dish, add the tomato wedges, kaffir lime leaves (lightly crushed in your palm) and the blistered onion and chillies. Cook for 2-3 minutes until the sauce thickens further and coats the beef. Taste and add more tamarind puree or sugar according to your taste.

NOTE: Gula melaka can be purchased from Asian grocery stores. It is sometimes known as gula jawa. This should not be replaced with palm sugar which is a lot lighter in colour and sweeter in flavour.

Dark Soy and Black Vinegar Braised Beef

SERVES 4-6

Braises are a great way to render off excess fat, particularly from cuts like beef rib or brisket. In this recipe, use either cut. Beef is a great choice for this dish as it can withstand the bold flavours of the dark soy and black vinegar. However, the right balance of flavours for the braising liquor is necessary.

1.5 kg (3.3 lbs) beef ribs on the bone, cleaned and excess fat trimmed off, cut into 10 cm (4 in) lengths. If you are using brisket, you can cook it as a whole piece
6 cloves garlic, crushed, skinned
15 g (0.5 oz) ginger, peeled, sliced thickly
2 small dried chillies
6 cloves
2 star anise
1 stick (6 cm, 2.3 in) cinnamon
½ teaspoon black peppercorns
60 ml (¼ cup) Shaoxing wine
60 ml (¼ cup) dark soy
60 ml (¼ cup) black vinegar
60 g (2 oz) rock sugar
2 tablespoons oil

In a large saucepan, heat 2 tablespoons of oil over high heat. Add the garlic, ginger, chillies, cloves, star anise, cinnamon and peppercorns and cook for 2 minutes.

Add the beef and brown all over. Deglaze with the Shaoxing wine, then add the dark soy, vinegar and rock sugar along with 1 cup of water.

Bring to the boil, then lower the heat and cook on low with the lid on for 2 hours or until the meat is very tender. You may need to add up to an extra ¼ cup of water if the sauce starts to dry up. This part of the cooking can be done in a pressure cooker. Cook on medium pressure for 45-50 minutes.

Raw Salmon, Herbs, Crispy Fish Skin and Szechuan Dressing

SERVES 4

I first made a version of this dish on Masterchef. It absolutely relies on using the freshest salmon and, in Australia, we are truly spoilt with incredibly fresh Tasmanian salmon. If you have yet to try crispy fish skin, this is a must. I'm big on using every bit of an ingredient and this is the perfect way to use fish skin. The dish is beautiful and makes an impression! Add a dash of my Szechuan Dressing and the entire dish is totally transformed.

600 g (1.3 lbs) fresh
  Atlantic/Tasmanian salmon
  fillet, skin on, pin boned
1 tablespoon olive oil
½ teaspoon smoked salt or sea salt
½ cup micro herbs (shiso,
  coriander, watercress)
1 large red chilli, deseeded,
  finely julienned
1 knob (10 g, 0.35 oz) young
  ginger, skinned, finely julienned
1 stalk spring onion, washed,
  trimmed and finely sliced on
  the diagonal
Crispy shallots, to taste

SZECHUAN DRESSING
1 teaspoon dou ban jiang (broad
  bean chilli paste)
1 tablespoon black vinegar
1 tablespoon dark soy sauce
Pinch of sugar
1 teaspoon water

Preheat the oven to 180°C (356°F).

Using a sharp filleting knife, barrel out the fish by running the knife lengthways from the middle of the fillet, down towards the skin (without cutting through the skin) and around towards the edge, ensuring the bloodlines are left on the skin. Repeat on the belly side of the salmon. Keep the fish flesh in the fridge.

To prepare the crispy fish skin, hold the knife at a slight angle, start from the middle and shave off all the remaining flesh from the skin. Repeat on the other side.

Place the skin on a tray lined with greaseproof paper. Drizzle over with the olive oil and rub on both sides of the fish skin, and place it back on the tray skin-side up and sprinkle on the smoked salt or sea salt. Place another layer of greaseproof paper over the top of the fish skin and weigh it down with another baking sheet. Bake for 20-25 minutes until golden and crispy. Remove from the oven, drain off excess oil and set aside on a wire rack to cool.

Slice each piece of fish about ½ cm thick and place on a serving plate.

Mix the dressing ingredients together in a small bowl, taste and adjust accordingly.

Just before serving, sprinkle the dressing over the fish slices and top with the herbs, chilli, ginger and spring onion, crispy shallots and small bits of the crispy fish skin. Serve immediately.

NOTE: This dish is best served slightly chilled. So remove the fish from the refrigerator just before slicing. The fish will also be firmer and easier to slice.

Shichimi Togarashi Crusted Tuna, Daikon and Salad

SERVES 4

While in Osaka, Japan, I came across an old noodle shop selling soba and udon. The chef, an old man, had been doing this for some 30 years and I loved that he was dedicated to perfecting a simple, yet complex-tasting dish. Being obsessed with chilli pepper, I doused my soba with his Shichimi Togarashi (seven-spice chilli peppers) powder. But there was something quite distinct about this particular one. Finally, it came to me, Szechuan peppercorns! In addition, his had a rather citrusy fragrance that was just amazing.

Inspired by "The Noodle Man in Osaka" and the wonderful tuna at the famous Tsukiji Fish Market in Tokyo, here is a really simple, healthy and delicious salad!

400 g (14 oz) fresh tuna steak, chilled

2 tablespoons Shichimi Togarashi (Japanese seven-spice chilli peppers)

½ teaspoon black sesame seeds

250 g (8.8 oz) daikon, peeled, finely shredded

1 stalk spring onion, finely sliced on the diagonal

½ cup coriander leaves, pick the baby leaves

VINAIGRETTE

3 tablespoons rice wine vinegar

1 tablespoon tamari

1 teaspoon finely diced young ginger

1 tablespoon finely sliced spring onion

¼ teaspoon sugar

Toast the sesame seeds on a dry frying pan over medium heat for a minute or 2 or until fragrant.

Slice the tuna into equal bite-sized pieces, about 1½ cm x 2 cm (0.6 x 0.8 in). Lightly coat with the Shichimi Togarashi pepper.

Mix the vinaigrette together in a small bowl.

In a separate mixing bowl, toss the daikon, spring onions, coriander leaves, black sesame with just enough dressing to coat.

Serve the tuna pieces with the salad and drizzle over a little more dressing.

Crispy Salmon Belly

SERVES 4

The Japanese love the fatty salmon belly which contains a huge amount of Omega-3 oils. If you're not a big fan, here's a very simple way of cooking this part of the fish which will make you want to eat an entire plateful!

600 g (1.3 lbs) salmon belly, pat dry and sliced into escalopes
Oil for deep frying

Heat the oil to about 180°C (356°F). Slowly lower pieces of salmon and fry for 2 minutes or until the edges are slightly golden and crisp. Drain on paper towels.

Serve with my Herb Salad (page 140) drizzled with Hot and Sour Dressing (page 170).

Raw Snapper with Shichimi Togarashi and Sesame Dressing

SERVES 4

If you've ventured around the hawker scene in Singapore, you would've come across stalls serving congee with the option of adding raw fish. Dig a little further and you'll find that they also serve a raw fish dish using Ikan Parang (Wolf Herring) with chillies, lime and iceberg lettuce. It is the most divine dish and relies on incredibly fresh fish. This dish works very well for dinner parties, either as an individual starter or as a shared plate. Here's my version of this wonderful dish.

240 g (8.5 oz) skinless fresh snapper fillet
½ cup finely shredded cabbage
1 knob (10 g, 0.35 oz) young ginger, peeled, finely shredded
2 stalks spring onion, finely sliced on the diagonal
1 hot red chilli, finely sliced on the diagonal
1 hot green chilli, finely sliced on the diagonal
Shichimi Togarashi (Japanese seven-spice chilli peppers), to taste

DRESSING
2 teaspoons light soy sauce or tamari
2 teaspoons fresh lime juice
2 teaspoons sesame oil
Pinch of sugar

Use a sharp knife and slice the fish very thinly across the grain at an angle. Place decoratively on a dish. Top with the cabbage, ginger, spring onions and chillies. Sprinkle with the Shichimi Togarashi and drizzle over the dressing just before serving.

NOTE: You can replace the snapper with any fresh, tender white fish that doesn't have too many bloodlines or sinews.

Family Favourites

Every family has its favourite dishes. Mine often revolve around dishes that are quick to cook, nourishing and super yummy. Then, in the weekends when time permits for a little more planning, I pull out the super scrummy dishes that might take just a little longer to cook. These are definitely my sons Alex's and Andre's favourite meals. So, on many occasions, each gets to choose what I cook. The importance of my heritage, living in Australia and my travels, feature strongly in what I cook for my family. In my mind, the joy of food is greatest when it can be shared with family.

My Dan Dan Topping

SERVES 4

This recipe resulted one day when I was cooking Spaghetti Bolognaise and wanted something Chinese and spicy instead. I had the lean minced beef, the French beans and always have a store of frozen chillies, garlic and fermented bean paste. So, I made a version of the topping for Dan Dan Mien, the spicy and meaty Szechuan noodles. It turned out delicious, perfect with steamed rice or tossed in with thin egg noodles.

500 g (1.1 lbs) lean minced beef

150 g (5 oz) French beans, finely chopped

3 cloves garlic, crushed, skinned, finely chopped

1 medium onion, peeled and finely chopped

1 red chilli, finely chopped

2 teaspoons fermented soy bean paste

2 teaspoons chilli bean paste

1 teaspoon white pepper

1 teaspoon dark soy sauce

2 sprigs fresh coriander, washed, roots and stems finely chopped, leaves roughly chopped

2 stalks spring onion, trimmed, finely sliced

1 teaspoon tapioca flour, mixed with 2 tablespoons water

2 tablespoons oil

1 Lebanese cucumber, thinly sliced and shredded

Heat a wok or medium saucepan over high heat and add 2 tablespoons of oil. Fry the garlic, onion and chilli for 1-2 minutes or until slightly softened. Add the beans and cook for a further 2 minutes.

Include the beef and cook for 2 to 3 minutes, stirring continuously to break up the lumps. Then add the fermented soy sauce beans, chilli bean paste, pepper, dark soy sauce, and coriander roots and stems. Stir to combine. Add the tapioca slurry and mix well.

Serve over steamed hot rice or egg noodles. Top with shredded cucumber, spring onions, chillies and coriander leaves.

NOTE: You can switch the beef with pork or chicken.

Wonton Soup

MAKES ABOUT 30-40

This is a staple in my house. It's quick to make, wholesome and creates a hearty meal for the family. Wonton soup also works well as a starter or simply served in a big bowl with a ladle and small bowls for sharing.

1 packet wonton wrappers,
    40 - 60 sheets

FILLING
250 g (8.8 oz) chicken mince
100 g (3.5 oz) prawn meat
2 large cabbage leaves (Chinese,
    white or Savoy)
½ teaspoon finely grated ginger
½ teaspoon white pepper
1 tablespoon light soy sauce
1 tablespoon Shaoxing wine
1 teaspoon oyster sauce
½ teaspoon sesame oil
¼ teaspoon sugar
1 teaspoon cornflour or tapioca
    flour

SOUP
1 litre (4.2 cups) good quality
    chicken stock
Greens (bok choy, choy sum or
    English spinach), trimmed to
    bite-sized lengths
2 stalks spring onion, finely
    sliced
Pepper (optional)
Crispy shallots
Sesame oil

To prepare the filling, lightly blanch the cabbage in boiling water. Remove and drain. Alternatively, microwave for 30 seconds. Wrap in a clean tea towel and squeeze out as much liquid as possible. Finely chop.

Combine all filling ingredients together in a glass or non-reactive bowl. Mix well and set aside.

Use each wonton wrapper to wrap ½ teaspoon of the filling. Set aside on a plate.

Bring a medium-sized pot of water to the boil. Blanch the greens in the boiling water. Remove and drain. Cook the wontons in the pot of boiling water until just cooked, approximately 2-3 minutes.

In a separate pot, bring the good quality chicken stock to the boil. Season with a little pepper if desired.

Place the greens and wontons in a bowl, pour over some hot chicken stock, sprinkle over some spring onions, crispy shallots and a few drops of sesame oil. Serve hot.

NOTE: To make it a more substantial meal, add some egg noodles cooked in boiling water until al dente.

There are many ways of wrapping wontons. One of my favourite ways is to use the back of a teaspoon to smear ½ a teaspoon of filling in the middle of the wrapper. Dab some water on the edges, fold it over into a triangle, pressing the edges firmly to seal. Dab the sealed edges of the resulting triangle with water, bring together and pinch to seal. The hollow in the middle of the wonton allows the hot soup to cook the wonton evenly.

Siu Mai

MAKES ABOUT 15-20

Yum-cha is one of my favourite meals to have. It's social and half the fun is in chasing down the trolleys serving the food you want. I always go for the steamed dumplings such as Siu Mai. These are quick and easy to make, and cooks in 6-7 minutes. Get the children involved in making their own dumplings for a fun, family activity.

FILLING
250 g (8.8 oz) chicken thigh fillet, coarsely minced
100 g (3.5 oz) prawn meat, coarsely chopped (optional)
2 leaves Chinese or white cabbage
2 dried shiitake mushrooms, rehydrated, finely chopped
$1/2$ teaspoon finely chopped ginger
2 stalks spring onion, finely chopped
$1/2$ teaspoon white pepper
1 tablespoon light soy sauce
1 teaspoon oyster sauce
1 tablespoon Shaoxing wine
$1/2$ teaspoon sesame oil
$1/4$ teaspoon sugar
1 teaspoon cornflour or tapioca flour

Wonton wrappers
$1/2$ carrot, finely diced

Remove the racks from a steamer, fill with water and bring to the boil.

Combine the chicken mince, prawn meat if using, and all filling ingredients in a glass bowl. Mix well. Set aside for 20 minutes.

Place 1 teaspoon of filling in the middle of each wrapper, gather up the sides leaving the top exposed. Garnish each Siu Mai with some diced carrot.

Line the steamer racks with perforated baking paper or spray lightly with oil. Steam for about 6-7 minutes or until cooked.

Serve immediately with chilli sauce.

Fried Brown Rice with Chilli, Ikan Bilis, Tofu and Kale

SERVES 4

This is an incredibly healthy and wholesome yet super-delicious dish combining all my favourite ingredients. For a purely vegetarian dish, exclude the ikan bilis.

2 cups cold cooked brown rice
3 eggs, lightly beaten
1 cup ikan bilis (dried anchovies), rinsed and drained
2 cloves garlic, peeled, finely chopped
2 red chillies, finely sliced
2 tablespoons laksa paste (page 160) (optional, or 1 tablespoon of your preferred chilli paste)
2 cups chopped kale
300 g (10.5 oz) tau kwa (fried fresh tofu), cut into ½ cm, 0.2 in cubes
2 tablespoons light soy sauce
½ teaspoon white pepper
Oil

Heat 4 tablespoons of oil in a wok over medium-high heat. Scramble the eggs until three-quarters cooked. Remove and set aside.

Add another 2 tablespoons of oil in the wok and fry the ikan bilis until crispy. Add the garlic, chillies and laksa paste if using, and fry for 1 minute.

Include the kale and fry until slightly wilted. Add the rice, tau kwa, light soy sauce and pepper and toss for a further 3 minutes. Taste and adjust seasoning to your liking. Return the eggs and toss to combine. Top with crispy shallots and serve hot.

NOTE: If you can't find tau kwa at your local Asian grocery, cut up some fresh tofu into small cubes and deep fry until golden and crispy.

Easy Peasy Fried Rice

SERVES 2-4

Fried Rice was one of the first dishes I learnt to cook at Home Economic class in school. It's a humble dish but one that can be so satisfying, not to mention the endless variations possible. It's also a great way to use up all sorts of leftovers. Use this recipe as a base and experiment with your own concoctions.

2 cups cold leftover cooked long-grain or Jasmine rice
2 eggs, lightly beaten
2 cloves garlic, peeled, finely chopped
1 small Spanish onion, peeled, finely diced
2 long red hot chillies, finely sliced
1 lap cheong (Chinese sausage), thinly sliced on the diagonal
1/4 cup finely sliced French beans
2 tablespoons soy sauce
1 teaspoon fermented soy beans (optional)
1/2 teaspoon white pepper
2 stalks spring onion, finely sliced
Crispy shallots
Oil

Break up the cooked rice with wet hands to remove any lumps.

Heat 2 tablespoons of oil in a wok or non-stick frying pan over medium-high heat. Scramble the eggs until three-quarters cooked. Remove and set aside.

Add 2 tablespoons of oil in the wok and fry the garlic, onion, chillies, lap cheong and beans for 2-3 minutes. Toss in the rice. Season with soy sauce, fermented beans if using, and pepper.

Return the eggs and include the spring onions, toss to combine. Taste and add salt to taste (keep in mind that the lap cheong is salty). Sprinkle over some crispy shallots and serve.

Baked Ricotta with Chilli Flakes

SERVES 4

This is an absolute winner of a dip and is so quick to make. I sometimes cook this up if I want something light for supper! It is so delicious served straight out of the oven with a crusty fresh baguette.

250 g (8.8 oz) fresh ricotta
Dried chilli flakes
Dried mint
Sea salt
Extra virgin olive oil

Preheat your oven to 180°C (356°F).

Place the ricotta in a small ovenproof ramekin or dish, top with a pinch of dried chilli flakes, dried mint, sea salt and a good glug of extra virgin olive oil. Cover with foil and bake in the oven for 15-20 minutes. Serve with fresh baguette.

Veal, Pork, Bacon and Leek Meatballs

SERVES 4

My children love tomato-based pasta dishes. Instead of the usual Spaghetti Bolognaise, these meatballs are different and fun to make with the kids! Veal is slightly lighter in flavour than beef. I often use a combination of beef and pork if veal is unavailable.

400 g (14 oz) freshly-made pasta or dried pasta (bucatini is a fun alternative to spaghetti)
Oil

MEATBALLS
250 g (8.8 oz) minced veal
250 g (8.8 oz) minced pork
2 rashes middle bacon, rind trimmed, chopped, pan fried until lightly golden, cooled
½ stalk large leek, washed well, finely chopped
6 cloves garlic, crushed, skin removed, finely chopped,
2 sprigs coriander leaves, finely chopped
1 tablespoon onion jam (optional)
1 teaspoon ground cumin
1 teaspoon sweet paprika
½ teaspoon dried chilli flakes, or to your liking
Cracked black pepper
½ teaspoon sugar
1 teaspoon salt
2 tablespoons breadcrumbs

TOMATO SAUCE
700 g (1.5 lbs) passata, puree or tinned crushed tomatoes
60 ml (¼ cup) red wine
Dried oregano
Pinch of sugar
Parmesan cheese, freshly grated
2 sprigs fresh parsley, roughly chopped

In a glass mixing bowl, mix the meatball ingredients together. Knead lightly until well combined, taking care not to compress the filling too much. Make round meatballs the size of golf balls; you should get about 18 -20. Set aside.

Heat 2-3 tablespoons of olive oil in a wide, non-stick saucepan over medium-high heat. Arrange the meatballs in a single layer and fry until nicely browned all over.

Pour in the passata, red wine and oregano. Fill the passata bottle with about ½ cup of water, shake well and pour into the saucepan. Lightly stir to avoid breaking up the meatballs. Cover and simmer for 20 minutes. Taste and adjust flavours with sugar and salt to your liking.

In the meantime, cook the pasta until al dente, drain and add directly to the sauce. Stir through, top with grated parmesan and chopped parsley and serve immediately.

Finger-Lickin' Crispy Chicken Ribs

SERVES 4

If you have yet to discover what chicken ribs are, visit your poultry supplier or local supermarket and ask for it. It's the cut that runs from the wing through to the neck of the chicken. It has a small, flat bone and lots of meat around it. Absolutely everyone who has had it at one of my pop-ups love it! I once had a bride's father station himself right outside the kitchen at his daughter's wedding just so he wouldn't miss out on the never-ending flow of ribs coming out of the kitchen!

1 kg (2.2 lbs) skinless chicken ribs
1 cup rice flour
1 teaspoon sea salt
Oil for deep frying

MARINADE
4 large stalks lemongrass, white
  parts only, sliced
2 knobs (20 g, 7 oz) turmeric
4 long hot red chillies
3 teaspoons smoked salt or
  sea salt
2 teaspoons brown sugar

In a food processor, finely grind the lemongrass, turmeric and chillies. Massage into the chicken along with the salt and sugar. Leave to marinade for a few hours or overnight in the fridge.

Heat the oil in a deep-fryer or large wok to 180°C (356°F).

Mix the rice flour and salt in a large mixing bowl. Dust the chicken pieces in the flour and deep fry until just cooked.

Serve hot with my Chilli Vinaigrette (page 169).

NOTE: If you can't find chicken ribs, chicken wings will suffice or, at a stretch, pieces of chicken thigh with excess fat trimmed off. The marinade can be altered by adding more or less chilli to your taste.

Slow-Roasted Pork Spare Ribs

SERVES 4-6

Spare ribs, often with soft bones and layers of fat through it, are a beautiful cut of pork to cook with. Marinating it well and cooking it for a long time results in really juicy, tender and flavoursome meat.

1.2 kg (2.6 lbs) pork spare ribs strip, skinless, cut into 6-8 cm (about 2.5-3 in) pieces, excess fat trimmed

2 tablespoons kecap manis (Indonesian sweet sauce)

MARINADE

1 teaspoon Szechuan peppercorn

$^1/_2$ teaspoon white peppercorn

4 cloves garlic, peeled, grated

10 g (0.35 oz) ginger, peeled, grated

2 sprigs fresh coriander, roots, stems, leaves, finely chopped

$^1/_2$ teaspoon chilli flakes

2 tablespoons olive oil

$2^1/_2$ tablespoons kecap manis (Indonesian sweet sauce)

$^1/_2$ teaspoon sea salt

To prepare the marinade, dry roast the Szechuan and white peppercorns in a frying pan over medium heat for about 2 minutes or until fragrant. Cool and grind in a mortar and pestle until fine. Place the ground pepper with all the other marinade ingredients together in a food processor and blitz well. Pour over the pork and rub in well. Cover with cling film and refrigerate overnight.

Preheat your oven to 180°C (356°F).

Place the marinated pork in an ovenproof baking dish or roasting pan. Cover snuggly with foil and roast for 1$^1/_2$ hours. Remove the foil and bake for a further 30 minutes, basting frequently with the pan liquid. Drizzle 2 tablespoons of kecap manis over the top of the pork and roast for a further 5-10 minutes until lightly charred and most of the pan juices have reduced.

Remove from the oven, cover loosely with foil and rest for 15 minutes. Slice into 1-2 cm slices and serve with hot, steamed rice.

Spiced Pulled Pork

SERVES 10-12

It's quite funny how food has its trends. These days, when pulled pork features on any cafe menu, quite likely it will be the go-to dish. This is one of the most popular dishes on my catering menu. Everyone loves it. It's served with a soft milk bread roll with finely-shredded cabbage and my Pickled Green Chilli Mayo. Simply to die for!

1 kg pork neck, cleaned, some but not all the fat trimmed

MARINADE

3 sprigs fresh coriander, trimmed, roughly chopped roots and all
1 heaped tablespoon of your favourite marmalade
3 cloves garlic, peeled
1 teaspoon smoked paprika
1 teaspoon ground cumin
½ teaspoon ground coriander
½-1 teaspoon ground chilli, to taste
1 teaspoon smoked salt or sea salt
1 tablespoon tomato paste
2 tablespoons raw sugar
2 tablespoons malt or balsamic vinegar
2 tablespoons olive oil

Place all the marinade ingredients in a food processor and blitz until smooth.

Place the meat in a glass or ceramic dish, pour over the marinade, squishing it into the meat. Cover with cling film and leave to marinate overnight in the fridge.

Preheat the oven to 170°C (338°F). Place the meat and all the marinade in an ovenproof baking dish, cover snugly with foil and bake for 2 hours.

Remove the foil, baste with the liquid at the bottom of the baking dish and bake uncovered at 180°C (356°F) for a further ½ hour. There should be excess liquid at the bottom of the dish. Taste this and adjust with more salt or sugar to your liking; this will be added to the pork.

Loosely cover the dish with foil and rest for 20-30 minutes. Use two large forks to shred the meat. Toss through the remaining liquid in the dish.

Serve your sliders with soft, mini milk rolls, my Pickled Green Chilli Mayo and finely shredded cabbage.

NOTE: My Pickled Green Chilli Mayonnaise is available from Hubers Butchery in Singapore at Dempsey. For stockists in Australia, please contact info@audramorrice.com.au.

Salmon Pie

SERVES 4

My kids love salmon and I'm so thankful for that! It is rich in Omega 3, so it's really good for you! I often find new ways of cooking it to keep it interesting. Here's a really simple recipe that is delicious and will wow even the most fussy eater. I sometimes add a layer of sauteed sliced button mushrooms into the mix. Think of this as Salmon Wellington!

600 g (1.3 lbs) skinless salmon fillet
3 cloves garlic, peeled, finely chopped
2 stalks spring onion, finely sliced
3 cups English spinach, roughly chopped
Smoked salt or sea salt
Pinch of sugar
Pinch of white pepper, freshly cracked
4 tablespoons full cream milk
½ teaspoon plain flour
Olive oil
2 sheets puff pastry
1 egg, lightly beaten for egg wash

Preheat your oven to 190°C (375°F). Line a baking sheet with greaseproof paper.

In a frying pan, heat 2 tablespoons of oil over medium-high heat. Add the garlic and fry for 30 seconds. Add the spring onions and cook for a further 30 seconds, then add the spinach.

Season with smoked salt, sugar, pepper, then add the milk. Stir well then sprinkle over the plain flour. Continue to stir to combine and cook for a further minute. Set aside to cool.

Lay the first sheet of pastry on the baking sheet. Place the salmon in the middle. Season with a pinch of smoked salt. Spoon over the spinach mixture and spread to cover the fillet. Cover with the other sheet of pastry and mould over the fish, sealing the overlapping pastry.

Cut the excess pastry around the fish and press with a fork to seal the edges. Brush lightly with egg wash and bake in the oven for 35-45 minutes until the pastry is golden, crispy and the fish is cooked through.

Rest for 5 minutes before slicing into portions. Serve with a leafy salad and my Basic Vinaigrette (page 169).

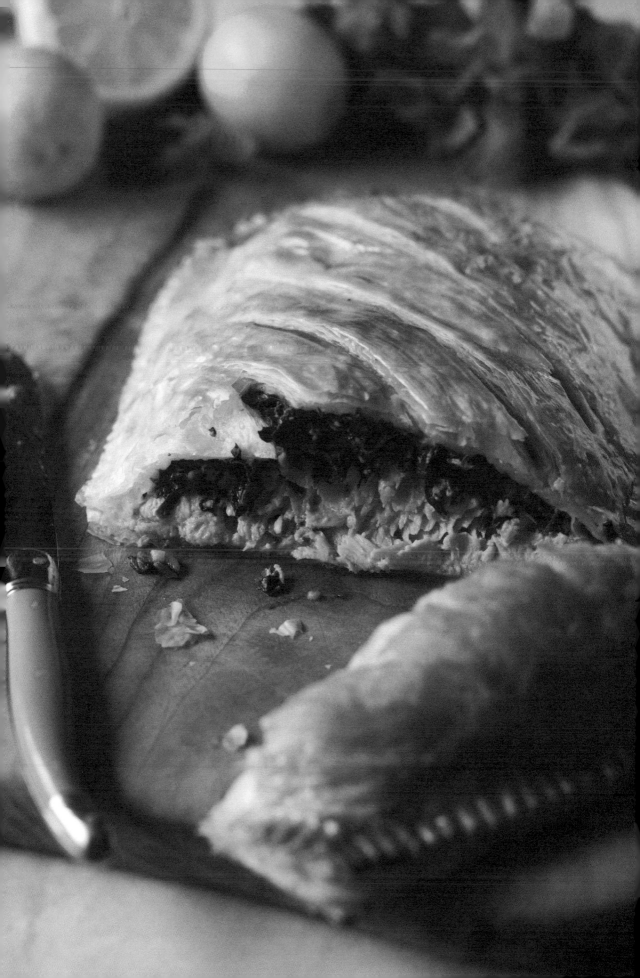

Baked Eggs

SERVES 4

Inspired by the Middle Eastern Shakshuka with its origins from Tunisia, this is one of the best ways to cook eggs. You can keep it really simple or make it a little more substantial by adding chorizo and beans. This is a standby dish for when I have to get a meal on the table instantly!

6 eggs
2 cloves garlic, peeled and finely
  chopped
2 cans of 440 g (15.5 oz) crushed
  tomatoes
½ teaspoon sweet paprika
½ teaspoon ground cumin
¼-1 teaspoon dried chilli flakes,
  or to your liking
½ teaspoon sugar
Pinch of salt
1 sprig fresh coriander, stems
  and leaves, roughly chopped
1-2 chorizo, chopped into small
  pieces (optional)
1 can (400 g, 14 oz) borlotti
  beans, drained (optional)
Olive oil

Heat 2 tablespoons of oil in a medium frying pan over medium-high heat. If you are using chorizo, fry in the frying pan until crispy. Remove and set aside.

Cook the garlic in the pan for 1 minute. Add the tomatoes, beans (if using), paprika, cumin, chilli flakes, sugar and salt. Stir and bring to the boil, then lower the heat and simmer for 5-6 minutes. Taste and adjust to your liking.

Make 6 holes in the tomato base in the pan and crack the eggs in the holes. Sprinkle over the chorizo, cover, and cook until the eggs are cooked to your liking. I tend to cook the whites through and leave the yolks runny!

Scatter with the chopped coriander and serve hot with fresh baguette.

Smoked Trout, Feta and Pea Tart

SERVES 6-8

Savoury tarts are one of those dishes that are both comforting and yet sophisticated, especially when you add the likes of smoked trout which gives a beautifully light, smokey flavour. This tart is simple to make, yet incredibly tasty and light! Whatever you do, don't over bake it. Look for the perfect wobble in the custard.

SOUR CREAM PASTRY
170 g (6 oz) plain flour
140 g (5 oz) butter
80 ml (⅓ cup) sour cream

FILLING
100-150 g (3.5 - 5.3 oz) hot
  smoked trout, flesh separated
50 g (1.8 oz) feta cheese, crumbled
1 stalk spring onion, finely
  chopped
100 g (3.5 oz) peas, fresh or
  frozen
400 ml (1.7 cups) thickened
  cream
3 eggs
Pinch of smoked salt or sea salt
Pinch of white pepper

To make the pastry, butter a 24 cm (9.5 in) loose-base tart tin and dust lightly with flour.

Place the flour and butter in a food processor. Pulse until the mixture resembles coarse breadcrumbs. With the motor running, add the sour cream and blitz until a dough forms. Remove the dough, flatten into a disc and wrap with cling film. Rest in the refrigerator for 20-30 minutes.

Preheat your oven to 180°C (356°F).

Roll out the dough between 2 sheets of greaseproof paper or a clean plastic sheet to 2 mm (almost 0.1 in) thick. Line the tart tin with the pastry, trimming off the edges.

Line the tart with foil or greaseproof paper, fill with uncooked rice or baking beads and blind bake for 20-30 minutes until lightly golden around the edges. Remove the beads and paper and bake for a further 5-10 minutes. Remove from the oven and set aside to cool.

For the filling, whisk together the cream, eggs, salt and pepper in a medium-sized bowl,

Place the tart tin on a baking tray. Fill the tart case with the smoked trout, feta and spring onions. Sprinkle over the peas, then pour in the cream and egg mixture. Do this with the tray sitting on the oven rack to avoid spillage.

Bake for 30 minutes or until the filling is just cooked and slightly wobbly. Let the tart rest for 10 minutes before removing from the tin. Serve with a leafy salad and my Basic Vinaigrette (page 169).

NOTE: In warmer climates, you may not need to add all the sour cream for the dough to come together. Start with 1 tablespoon, blitz, and as soon as the dough comes together, it is ready. Working on the pastry in a cool room will make it easier to manage.

You can make mini party tarts with mini tart/brioche tins with this recipe.

Alex's and Andre's Favourite Pancakes

SERVES 4

My kids look forward to weekends when we have a little more time to enjoy home-cooked pancakes. I picked up a tip from a chef friend who suggested I separate the eggs and finish off the pancakes in the oven to create an almost souffle texture to my pancakes. These are soft and fluffy and incredibly delicious.

250 g (1 cup) fresh ricotta
250 ml (1 cup) buttermilk
4 eggs, separated
Pinch of salt
1 heaped tablespoon sugar
150 g (1 cup) flour
1 teaspoon baking powder
Fresh blueberries or bananas
    peeled and sliced on the
    diagonal
Honey or maple syrup
Butter

Sift together the flour and baking powder.

Mix the ricotta, buttermilk, egg yolks, salt and sugar in a large bowl. Fold in the flour. In a separate bowl, whisk the egg whites until soft peaks. Gently fold into the batter, then fold in the blueberries.

Lightly grease a non-stick pan with butter and place over medium heat. Add 2-3 tablespoon spoons of batter to the pan and cook until bubbles appear. Flip over, then finish off the cooking in the oven for a further 2 minutes.

Serve with honey or maple syrup and whipped butter. If you are using bananas, stack them on top of the pancakes.

NOTE: To make whipped butter, simply whisk room temperature butter until light and fluffy. Then fold in maple syrup or honey or even crumbled up honeycomb and refrigerate until ready to use. If you like to shape them into a roll, refrigerate the butter until firm but still mouldable. Use cling film to shape the butter into a roll, twist to secure the ends and refrigerate until ready to use. Simply slice into pieces and place on top of the hot pancakes!

Corn Fritters

SERVES 4

Corn fritters are a breakie-brunch staple in my family. They are quick and easy to make, and very wholesome. You can use tinned corn if you wish – just make sure that the liquid is drained out completely. However, using fresh corn just adds to the crispness of the fritter!

3 raw, fresh whole corn on the cob
1 small Spanish onion, finely diced
2 sprigs coriander, including stems and roots, finely chopped
1 red chilli, seeds removed, finely diced
2 eggs
2-3 tablespoons plain flour
1 teaspoon smoked salt or sea salt
Pinch of sugar (omit if your corn is sweet)
Olive oil

Cook the corn, husk on, in the microwave for 6-8 minutes or until cooked through. Let it cool, remove the husk and slice off the kernels.

Mix everything together in a bowl, ensuring a slightly wet mixture, enough for the corn to stick together.

Add 2-3 tablespoons of oil in a non-stick pan over medium heat. Ladle on 2 tablespoons of corn batter and cook both sides until golden.

Serve with a big bunch of rocket dressed with a squeeze of lemon juice and extra virgin olive oil.

Chilli, Avocado, Egg Sarnie

SERVES 4

There are days when you just want something quick, easy, wholesome and delicious. This sarnie is something that we love in my family and I often make it for weekend lunches.

4 fresh brioche buns or 8 slices
  sourdough rye bread
4-6 free-range eggs
1 avocado, peeled, deseeded,
  thinly sliced
1 long hot red chilli, thinly sliced
  on the diagonal
Audra's Pickled Green Chilli
  Mayonnaise
Cracked black pepper
Pinch of smoked salt
Rocket leaves
Oil

Toast the bread and set aside.

Heat a non-stick frying pan with 2 tablespoons of oil over medium-high heat. Cook the eggs to your liking and scatter the chillies, black pepper and salt over the top.

Smother the toasted bread with Audra's Pickled Green Chilli Mayonnaise, top with the chilli, egg, avocado and rocket and tuck in!

NOTE: My Pickled Green Chilli Mayonnaise is available from Hubers Butchery in Singapore at Dempsey. For stockists in Australia, please contact info@audramorrice.com.au.

Salads & Greens

I can't say it more simply than "I love vegetables!" I could quite easily become a vegetarian if I had access to a whole host of vegetables, chillies, garlic and oyster sauce... okay, maybe, semi-vegetarian. With the range of vegetables grown these days, there are millions of delicious dishes you can cook to create a feast! Here are some of my favourites.

Sambal Kangkong

SERVES 4

Kangkong, also known as water spinach, river spinach, water morning glory, or water convolvulus is really easy to cook! Thinking about kangkong fried with blachan and chillies immediately makes my mouth water. It's so quick to cook and so delicious! Make sure you drain the veg well after washing and you'll definitely need very high heat to cook this well!

500 g (1.1 lbs) kangkong, chopped to 6 cm (2.5 in) lengths
3 cloves garlic, peeled, finely chopped
1 long red hot chilli, sliced on the diagonal
1 teaspoon (10 g, 0.35 oz) blachan (shrimp paste or Thai gapi)
Pinch of smoked salt (optional)
Pinch of sugar
Oil

Heat 2 tablespoons of oil in a wok over high heat. Add the blachan, breaking up with a spatula and cook for a minute until fragrant. Add the garlic and chilli and fry until the chillies are lightly blistered.

Put in the kangkong and toss until just wilted. Taste and add the sugar and a pinch of salt to your taste.

NOTE: When cooking kangkong, it is really important to cook it quickly and on very high heat.

Herb Salad

SERVES 4

This herb salad is incredibly versatile. Serve it with my Crispy Salmon Belly (page 106) or with my Smoked Salt, Avocado Oil Angus Rump (page 77). Or add some glass noodles and deep-fried fresh tofu for something vegetarian.

1 cup coriander leaves
1 cup mint leaves
1 cup Thai basil leaves
1 small Spanish onion, peeled, thinly sliced
1 Lebanese cucumber, halved lengthways, sliced on the diagonal

Mix all ingredients together and serve with my Hot and Sour Dressing (page 170).

French Beans, Blistered Chilli and Kecap Manis

SERVES 4

I consider beans to be one of those vegetables that are quite "meaty" and very high in protein. They make a great side dish but also serve well as a stand-alone feature in a banquet. The blistered chillies and kecap manis add a little heat, saltiness and sweetness that just makes it so much more scrumptious!

500 g (1.1 lbs) French beans, trimmed
2 cloves garlic, peeled, finely chopped
1 long red chilli, chopped
2 tablespoons kecap manis (Indonesian sweet sauce)
Oil

Heat 2 tablespoons of oil in a wok over high heat. Add the garlic and chillies and fry until the chillies are lightly blistered. Include the French beans and toss along with 1 tablespoon of water.

Cover, and cook for 2 minutes. Add the kecap manis and toss for a further 2 minutes or until the beans have softened but still a little crunchy.

Sambal Ladies Fingers (Okra)

SERVES 4

Ladies fingers or okra are quite commonly used in many cuisines of Southeast Asia through to India and North Africa. Cook them whole for a beautiful look or slice them for a quick stir-fry. Note that once they are sliced, they tend to get a little slimy but are still delicious. This is a really simple recipe with flavours of my Basic Sambal and small prawns to sweeten the dish. Absolutely divine!

300 g (10.5 oz) ladies fingers (okra), stems trimmed, sliced thickly on the diagonal
200 g (7 oz) small prawns, shelled
2 cloves garlic, peeled, finely chopped
2 tablespoons Basic Sambal (page 160)
1/2 teaspoon salt, or to taste
1/2 teaspoon sugar
Oil

Slice the ladies fingers into 1 cm (about 0.5 in) thick pieces on the diagonal.

Heat 2 tablespoons of oil in a wok or frying pan over high heat. Fry the garlic till fragrant, add the ladies fingers and toss for 1 minute. Include the prawns, sambal, salt and sugar. Toss until just cooked.

Gai Lan, Chilli, Crispy Garlic with Oyster Sauce

SERVES 4

Sometimes, the simplest of dishes is the most satisfying. This is one of them, simply tossed in oyster sauce and crispy garlic and blistered chillies. If there is one vegetable stir-fry for your repertoire, this is it!

400 g (14 oz) gai lan (Chinese broccoli), trimmed to 8 cm (3 in) lengths, separate the stems and leaves
3 cloves garlic, peeled, finely chopped
2 teaspoons oyster sauce
¼ teaspoon cornflour or tapioca flour (optional)
Oil

Bring a medium-sized pot of water to the boil. Blanch the stems and leaves of the gai lan separately as the stems will require a little more cooking. Drain well.

Heat 2 tablespoons of oil in a wok over high heat. Add the garlic and fry for 1 minute. Add the gai lan, stems and leaves, and the oyster sauce and toss. Mix the cornflour, if using, with 2 teaspoons of water. Stir into the dish and continue tossing to mix it through.

Sambal Asparagus

SERVES 4

If you've only ever had steamed or blanched asparagus with garlic and olive oil, venture my way and try this recipe. It's simple and super delicious!

450 g (1 lb) asparagus, woody ends removed
2 cloves garlic, peeled, finely chopped
1-2 tablespoons Basic Sambal (page 160)
½ teaspoon salt, or to taste
½ teaspoon sugar
Oil

Heat 2 tablespoons of oil in a wok over high heat. Add the asparagus, toss until just tender.

Add 1 tablespoon of sambal (or more if you like), salt and sugar. Toss to combine.

Sayor Lodeh

SERVES 4-6

This is one vegetarian dish that I cook often for friends and family, and for events. It's rich and coconuty but at the same time light with the separation of the coconut milk. There are lots of versions and mine includes all the vegetables I love to eat – including Brussels sprouts!

4 tablespoons The Absolute Mother of All Sambals (page 160)

15 g (0.5 oz) dried shrimp, soaked in water, drained and ground (optional)

500 ml (2 cups) coconut milk

½ cup good quality chicken stock

1 teaspoon sugar or to taste

1½ teaspoon salt or to taste

Oil

8 tau pok (dried tofu puffs), halved on the diagonal

200 g (7 oz) cabbage, cut into bite-sized pieces

150 g (5.3 oz) Brussels sprouts, trimmed, halved

150 g (5.3 oz) carrots, peeled, sliced into bite-sized pieces

150 g (5.3 oz) snake beans, cut into 6 cm (2.5 in) lengths

25 g (about 1 oz) tung hoon (glass noodles), soaked in water to soften, cut into half

150 g (5.3 oz) cauliflower, cut into florets

100 g (3.5 oz) tau kwa (fried tofu), cut into 2 x 4 cm (1 x 2 in) pieces

Fry the sambal in 3 tablespoons oil. Add the dried shrimp if using, and cook for a further 2 minutes until fragrant.

Add the coconut milk along with ½ cup of chicken stock. Bring to the boil.

Include all the vegetables, tau pok and vermicelli except for the cauliflower and tau kwa. Cook for 2-3 minutes. Then add the cauliflower and tau kwa.

Lower the heat to medium and cook until all the vegetables are tender. Season with the sugar and salt to taste.

NOTE: Dried shrimps add another flavour element to this dish. However, it can be left out.

Spicy, Sweet and Sour Szechuan Eggplant

SERVES 4

Eggplants carry the flavours that you add to it. It is important that you cook the eggplant to soften it first for a delicious result. So, either deep fry or steam them prior to flavouring. I absolutely love this dish. It's one that has been cooked in my family for decades and I never get tired of it.

500 g (1.1 lbs) eggplants (brinjal), stems trimmed, cut into 4 cm (1.5 in) thick wedges
3 cloves garlic, peeled, finely chopped
1 knob (10 g, 0.35 oz) ginger, peeled, finely julienned
2 large red chillies, slit into half lengthways
1 small Spanish onion, peeled, halved and cut into wedges
2 ripe tomatoes, cut into wedges
2 stalks spring onion, cut into 4 cm (1.5 in) lengths
Oil for deep-frying

SAUCE
2 tablespoons Shaoxing wine
2 tablespoons dou ban jiang (chilli bean paste)
3 tablespoons brown rice vinegar
1 tablespoon soy sauce
60 g (2 oz) rock sugar, crushed, pounded till fine
1/2 teaspoon Szechuan pepper

Heat the oil in a wok or deep-fryer to 180°C (356°F). Fry the eggplant in batches until golden. Drain on paper towels.

In a bowl, make the sauce by mixing together the Shaoxing wine, chilli bean paste, vinegar, soy, sugar and Szechuan pepper.

Remove all the oil from the wok except for 1 tablespoon. Add the garlic, ginger, chillies, onions, tomatoes, spring onions and fry on high heat for 1 minute.

Pour in the sauce and bring to the boil. Return the eggplants into the wok and toss to combine. Cook for a further 2 minutes.

Chicken and Crispy Noodle Slaw

SERVES 4-8

I've never been a huge salad person but in saying that, I do love a good colourful coleslaw with an Asian vinaigrette. Include chicken and store-bought crispy noodles and you instantly turn it into a reasonably substantial meal.

SALAD

250 g (8.8 oz) finely shredded
   Savoy cabbage
125 g (4.4 oz) carrots, peeled,
   thinly sliced on the diagonal
   and finely julienned
½ Spanish onion, peeled, thinly
   sliced
2 sprigs fresh coriander leaves,
   roughly chopped
½ cooked roast/poached chicken,
   deboned, meat shredded
50 g (1.8 oz) crispy noodles
   (store-bought)
2 tablespoons coarsely ground
   roasted peanuts
2 tablespoons crispy shallots
1 tablespoon crispy garlic

SESAME SOY DRESSING

4 teaspoons soy sauce
3 teaspoons brown rice vinegar
1½ teaspoons sesame oil
4 teaspoons olive oil
2 teaspoons sweet chilli sauce
1 teaspoon lemon juice

Combine the salad ingredients and toss with the dressing.

NOTE: If you don't have brown rice vinegar, replace with white wine vinegar, white vinegar, red wine vinegar or apple cider vinegar. You may need to balance the acidity by adjusting the sweetness with more sweet chilli sauce or by adding a little sugar. To make it gluten free, replace with gluten free soy or tamari. White cabbage can also be used.

For a basic Asian coleslaw, exclude the chicken and crispy noodles and for more colour, use purple cabbage. You can also dress with my Hot and Sour Dressing (page 170).

Betel Leaves with Dried Figs, Pomelo and Fresh Herbs

SERVES 4

This is a beautiful Thai-inspired vegetarian canapé I created for an event and everyone absolutely loved it. It's fresh and delightful, and wonderful to serve at parties! You can substitute the figs with some hot, smoked salmon for an equally delicious dish.

8 betel leaves, cleaned
2 tablespoons diced dried figs
2 tablespoons pomelo flesh, broken up
2 tablespoons finely diced daikon
2 tablespoons finely diced cucumber
1 tablespoon finely chopped fresh coriander
1 tablespoon finely chopped mint
½ teaspoon finely diced red chillies
1 tablespoon roasted peanuts, coarsely ground
1 tablespoon crispy shallots

DRESSING
1 tablespoon (20 g) tamarind pulp
1½ tablespoons (25 g) gula melaka (coconut sugar), shaved

To prepare the tamarind puree for the dressing, soak the pulp in 150 ml (½ cup) warm water until it softens, massage the pulp with your fingers to loosen, then use a sieve and press out as much puree as possible.

To make the dressing, place the tamarind puree and gula melaka in a small saucepan and bring to the boil. Stir until the gula melaka has dissolved. Strain and return it to the saucepan. Continue to simmer until the dressing has slightly thickened and becomes syrupy. Set aside to cool.

To make the topping, mix together the figs, pomelo, daikon, cucumber, coriander, mint and red chillies. Drizzle in 2 tablespoons of dressing and toss gently to combine.

Place the betel leaves onto a serving plate. Place about 1 tablespoon of topping on the middle of each betel leaf. Top with a little more dressing, a little ground peanuts and crispy shallots. Serve immediately.

To maintain it's freshness and crispness, this dish is best assembled and dressed just before serving.

NOTE: It is important to keep all the ingredients of a similar size to create a beautiful little morsel.

Avocado Salad

This is an incredibly healthy and delicious salad. Use a beautiful platter to make it look outstanding. This is a real show-stopper!

2 avocados, halved, deseeded, peeled
1 stalk spring onion, trimmed, thinly sliced on the diagonal
1 long red chilli, thinly sliced on the diagonal
50 g (1.8 oz) toasted almond flakes
Crispy shallots

Prepare a beautiful large serving platter.

Slice the avocados into thin, long wedges and place haphazardly on the platter. Scatter over the spring onions, chillies, almond flakes and crispy shallots.

Just before serving, drizzle over my Basic Vinaigrette (page 169).

Raw Mushroom Salad

SERVES 4

For someone who does not particularly fancy raw mushrooms, I absolutely love this dish. The dressing almost wilts the mushrooms and, like sponges, they soak up all the beautiful tart and tangy flavours. Serve this with my Smoked Salt, Avocado Oil Angus Rump (page 77) for a perfect meal!

100 g (3.5 oz) fresh cloud ear fungus or rehydrated dried wood ear fungus
150 g (5.3 oz) fresh inoki mushrooms
150 g (5.3 oz) fresh oyster/pearl mushrooms
150 g (5.3 oz) fresh shiitake mushrooms, sliced and pickled
4 small red radishes, trimmed, halved and thinly sliced
2 sprigs coriander leaves, picked

DRESSING
1 large sweet orange, zest and juice
3½ tablespoons tamari or premium soy sauce
1½ teaspoons dark soy sauce
3½ tablespoons brown rice vinegar
4 shallots, peeled, thinly sliced
1 tablespoon brown sugar
1 teaspoon sesame oil

In a large mixing bowl, tear mushrooms into strips, toss in the pickled mushrooms, radish and coriander leaves.

Dress the salad just before serving.

NOTE: See page 166 for how to pickle mushrooms.

Cumin-Roasted Sweet Potato, Toasted Pine Nuts, Chilli and Baby Spinach Salad

SERVES 4

This salad is quite substantial and a beautiful accompaniment to any barbecued or roasted beef or lamb.

350 g (12.3 oz) sweet potato, peeled, diced to 1 cm (0.4 in)
1 teaspoon cumin seeds, dry roasted in a frying pan
1 teaspoon smoked salt
Olive oil
1 long hot red chilli, finely diced
100 g (3.5 oz) baby spinach
50 g (1.8 oz) toasted pine nuts
100 g (3.5 oz) Greek feta
2-3 tablespoons pomegranate molasses or to taste
2 pinches of sumac or to taste

Preheat your oven to 180°C (356°F).

In a mixing bowl, toss together the sweet potato, cumin, salt and a couple of glugs of olive oil to lightly coat. Pour onto a baking tray lined with greaseproof paper and bake for 30 minutes or until lightly golden and tender.

In a salad dish, toss together the spinach and roasted sweet potato. Top with pine nuts and feta. Sprinkle over the sumac and drizzle over a little of the pomegranate molasses and some olive oil.

NOTE: If you can't find pomegranate molasses, use balsamic glaze with a squeeze of lemon juice.

Flavours

Open any Asian fridge or pantry and 9 out of 10 will be stocked with at least half a dozen, if not more, of sambals, pickles and sauces. As I write this, I have in my fridge, two huge jars of homemade pickles, pickled green chillies, sambals, my Fresh Red Chilli Relish... and the list goes on.

Many of these are staples and they are brought out when needed. The best thing about making your own is the fact that there aren't any preservatives added.

Sambals are the basis of a lot of my cooking. A sambal is basically a spice paste that incorporates chillies. The great thing about most sambals is that you can adjust the quantities of many of the ingredients to suit your taste.

Basic Sambal

MAKES 1 CUP

This is your base sambal and can be used for just about anything. My favourite is to add it as a base for stir-frying vegetables such as snake beans and asparagus!

SPICE PASTE

30 (30 g, 1 oz) long dried red chillies, soaked in hot water to rehydrate, drained

2 fresh long hot red chillies

1 large onion or 20 small shallots

1 teaspoon blachan (shrimp paste or Thai gapi), wrapped in foil and dry roasted in a pan over low-medium heat for 2 minutes until fragrant

Pinch of sea salt
Pinch of sugar
¼ cup oil

Grind all ingredients to a paste in a mortar and pestle, or food processor.

In a small saucepan, heat ¼ cup of oil over low-medium heat, add the spice paste and fry until fragrant or the oil separates, 8-10 minutes. Add the sea salt and sugar. Be sure to stir occasionally so it doesn't burn. Cool and store in a tightly sealed jar in the fridge or freezer.

Laksa Spice Paste

MAKES 1½ CUPS

30 g (1 oz) long dried red chillies, soaked in hot water, drained

4 fresh long hot red chillies

2 medium onions (240 g, ½ lb) or equivalent weight of shallots

4 cloves garlic, crushed, skinned

4 candlenuts

1 knob (10 g, 0.35 oz) galangal, roughly chopped

1 knob (10 g, 0.35 oz) fresh turmeric or 1 teaspoon turmeric powder

1 teaspoon (10 g, 0.35 oz) blachan (shrimp paste or Thai gapi), wrapped in foil and dry roasted in a pan for 2 minutes till fragrant

2 stalks lemongrass, white parts only, roughly chopped

Grind all ingredients to a paste in a mortar and pestle, or food processor.

In a medium saucepan, heat ¼ cup of oil over medium heat, add the spice paste and fry until fragrant.

Cool and store in a tightly sealed jar in the fridge or freezer.

Red Curry Paste

MAKES 1 CUP

½ teaspoon white peppercorns

¼ teaspoon cumin seeds

½ teaspoon coriander seeds

15 long dried red chillies, soaked
  in water and drained

½ knob (5 g, 0.17 oz) galangal,
  roughly chopped

½ knob (5 g, 0.17 oz) turmeric,
  roughly chopped

1 stalk lemongrass, white part
  only, roughly chopped

½ kaffir lime, zest finely chopped

2 coriander roots, finely chopped

5 cloves garlic, peeled

5 small shallots or 1 large onion

1 small hot red chilli (chilli padi,
  bird's eye chilli, optional)

½ teaspoon shrimp paste (Thai
  gapi or blachan)

Dry roast the peppercorns, cumin and coriander until fragrant. Cool and grind to a powder.

Using a mortar and pestle, or a blender, grind this powder and all the other curry paste ingredients together to a fine paste.

Cool and store in a tightly sealed jar in the fridge or freezer.

NOTE: Use this paste for your favourite red curry recipe with prawns, chicken or vegetables.

Green Curry Paste

MAKES 1 CUP

¼ teaspoon coriander seeds, toasted

¼ teaspoon cumin seeds, toasted

¼ teaspoon white peppercorns, toasted

2-4 long hot green chillies, roughly chopped

4 wild green chillies, roughly chopped

2 stalks lemongrass, white part only, roughly chopped

1 knob (10 g, 0.35 oz) galangal, roughly chopped

1 knob (10 g, 0.35 oz) turmeric, roughly chopped

1 medium Spanish onion or 10 shallots, peeled, roughly chopped

4 coriander roots, cleaned and roughly chopped

4 cloves garlic, peel

1 kaffir lime, zest

1 teaspoon Thai gapi (shrimp paste or blachan), wrapped in foil and roasted in the oven or in a dry pan over low-medium heat for 2 minutes or till fragrant

Grind all the ingredients together in a mortar and pestle or blitz in a food processor until a fine paste is formed.

Cool and store in a tightly sealed jar in the fridge or freezer.

NOTE: Wild green chillies are thin, slender green chillies, usually about 6 cm long. They provide great flavour and gives a good punch of heat. If unavailable, substitute with green chilli padi or green Thai bird's eye. Always check the level of heat to ensure it's not too overpowering.

The Absolute Mother of All Sambals

MAKES 1½ CUPS

I've probably said this in about 99 percent of the recipes in this book but this is truly my favourite sambal. There is always a batch of this sitting in both my fridge and freezer. I often use it as a base for a seafood sambal dish or simply to blob it over hot rice and a simple onion and chilli omelette. Try dunking chunks of cold cucumber into the sambal for a crazy but yummy snack!

SPICE PASTE

30 g (1 oz) long dried red chillies, rehydrated in hot water, drained
2 fresh red chillies
240 g (8.5 oz) onions or equivalent weight of shallots
4 candlenuts
1 knob (10 g, 0.35 oz) galangal, roughly chopped
1 knob (10 g, 0.35 oz) fresh turmeric or 1 teaspoon turmeric powder
1 teaspoon (10 g, 0.35 oz) blachan (shrimp paste or Thai gapi), wrapped in foil and dry roasted in a pan over low-medium heat for 2 minutes or until fragrant
2 stalks lemongrass, white part only, roughly chopped

60 ml (¼ cup) oil

Grind all ingredients to a paste in a mortar and pestle, or food processor. If you are using a mortar and pestle, start with the woodier ingredients like the galangal and lemongrass.

In a saucepan, heat ¼ cup of oil over low-medium heat, add the spice paste and fry until fragrant, about 8 to 10 minutes. You may need another 2 tablespoons of oil to cook down the sambal.

Cool and store in a tightly sealed jar in the fridge or freezer.

NOTE: To use this as a condiment, add 2 tablespoons of tamarind puree and 1 tablespoon of shaved gula melaka (coconut sugar), a pinch of salt and cook till disolved.

To prepare the tamarind puree, soak 1 tablespoon of tamarind pulp in 125 ml (½ cup) warm water until it softens. Massage the pulp with your fingers to loosen and dissolve the tamarind, then sieve to discard the seeds.

Quick Pickled Vegetables

MAKES A 750 ML (2 LB) JAR

Pickled veggies are certainly a brilliant side-serving and often help cut through the richness of any dish.

2 carrots, peeled, sliced
2 Lebanese cucumbers, sliced on
   the diagonal into long pieces
2 large red chillies, slit into half
   lengthways

PICKLING LIQUOR
125 ml (½ cup) water
125 ml (½ cup) white vinegar
110 g (½ cup) sugar
Pinch of salt
4 cloves

Bring the water, vinegar, sugar, salt and cloves to the boil until the sugar has melted. Boil for a further 2 minutes to reduce slightly. Remove from heat and set aside to cool.

Place the prepared carrot and cucumber in a clean mixing bowl or sterilised jar. Add the chilli and pour the pickling liquor over and let it marinate. These keep for only a few days in the fridge so make them as you plan to eat them.

Pickled Mushrooms

MAKES ABOUT 1½ CUPS

250 g (8.8 oz) fresh shiitake
   mushrooms

PICKLING LIQUOR
125 ml (½ cup) white vinegar
110 g (½ cup) sugar
125 ml (½ cup) water
Pinch of salt

Place all the pickling liquor ingredients in a saucepan over high heat. Bring to the boil and continue to boil until the liquor is sightly reduced. Remove from heat and set aside to cool.

Slice the mushrooms into 3 mm (0.1 in) thickness. Place in a ceramic or glass bowl and pour the pickling liquor over the mushrooms. Leave to marinate for 20 minutes.

Pickled Green Chillies

MAKES ABOUT 1½ CUPS

I always have a jar of these in my fridge, pulling it out when I've cooked up any type of noodles.

10 long hot green chillies, washed and dried, sliced into 2 mm (0.8 in) rings

PICKLING LIQUOR
125 ml (½ cup) white vinegar
110 g (½ cup) sugar
125 ml (½ cup) water
Pinch of salt
4 cloves

Place all the pickling liquor ingredients in a saucepan over high heat. Bring to the boil and continue to boil until the liquor is sightly reduced. Remove from heat and set aside to cool.

Place the chillies in a 500 ml (2 cup) sterilised glass jar. Pour over the cooled pickling liquor, cover tightly and refrigerate. This will store in the refrigerator for a month.

NOTE: You can always top up the pickling liquor with more freshly sliced green chillies. Make sure that the green chillies are washed well and dried entirely. Use a clean utensil when spooning out the chillies.

Fresh Red Chilli Relish

MAKES ABOUT 1 CUP

This is a must as an accompaniment to my Chicken Rice (page 25). It also works well with most of my roasted pork and duck recipes and my Soy-Braised Pork Belly (page 56).

10 fresh large hot red chillies
1 clove garlic
1 teaspoon sugar
Pinch of salt
1 lemon, zest and juice
½ teaspoon apple cider vinegar

Using a mortar and pestle, or a mini food processor, pound or blend the chillies, garlic, sugar and salt until mushy. Add the rest of the ingredients and mix well.

Taste and adjust according to your preference. Store in the refrigerator.

Achar

MAKES 2.5 LITRE JAR OF PICKLES

Penang achar tops my list of pickles. They are so incredibly moreish. My mother used to make jars and jars of them starting off with kilos of vegetables! This is particularly labour-intensive but worth every drop of sweat!

1.2 kg (2.6 lbs) telegraph cucumber, cut into 6 cm (2.5 in) logs, then quartered, seeds sliced off, and further halved into 8 sticks per log

500 g (1.1 lbs) carrots, peeled, cut into 6 cm (2.5 in) logs, then cut into 8 lengthwise for larger carrots or 4 for more slender carrots

400 g (14 oz) cauliflower, cut into bite-sized pieces

400 g (14 oz) cabbage, cut into bite-sized pieces

50 g (about ⅓ cup) roasted, coarsely ground peanuts

30 g (1 oz) white sesame seeds, toasted

PICKLING SAUCE

3 cloves garlic, crushed, skin removed

2 slices galangal

1 stalk lemongrass, white part only

1 knob (10 g, 0.35 oz) turmeric

15 long dried red chillies

4 large fresh hot red chillies

250 ml (1 cup) vinegar

160 g (5.6 oz) sugar

5 g (0.2 oz) salt

125 g (1 cup) roasted, coarsely ground peanuts

Oil

BLANCHING LIQUID

1 litre (4 cups) water

125 ml (½ cup) white vinegar

3 teaspoons of salt

To make the pickling sauce, blitz the garlic, galangal, lemongrass, turmeric, dried and fresh chillies together in a food processor or grind in a mortar and pestle to form a paste.

In a saucepan, heat 2 tablespoons of oil over medium heat, add the paste and cook for about 3 minutes, stirring frequently. Add the vinegar, sugar, salt and cook for about 2-3 minutes until the sugar dissolves. Mix in 1 cup of ground peanuts. Mix well, remove from the heat and set aside to cool.

In a large pot, mix together 1 litre (4 cups) of water, 125 ml (½ cup) of white vinegar, 3 teaspoons of salt and bring to the boil. Blanch each vegetable separately for no more than 20 seconds. Drain, place onto a clean tea towel and squeeze out any excess liquid. Place in a large mixing bowl.

When all the vegetables are done, mix in the pickling sauce along with the extra peanuts and sesame seeds. Store in a clean, sterilised glass jar and refrigerate for a couple of days before serving.

Ginger and Shallot Relish

MAKES ½ CUP

This is another perfect accompaniment to my Chicken Rice (page 25)!

2 knobs (20 g, 0.7 oz) ginger, peeled and grated
4 stalks spring onion, trimmed, use the white and light green part only, finely chopped
8 teaspoons hot water or chicken stock
Pinch of salt
4 teaspoons vegetable oil

Mix all ingredients except the oil in a small mixing bowl.

Heat the oil until piping hot, then pour over and mix well.

Basic Vinaigrette

MAKES ½ CUP

4 teaspoons apple cider vinegar
2 teaspoon Dijon mustard
1 teaspoon honey or maple syrup
2 teaspoon lemon juice
6 tablespoons light olive oil, avocado or any neutral flavoured oil (grapeseed, vegetable)

Whisk together the vinegar, mustard, maple syrup or honey, and lemon juice. Continue to whisk and slowly drizzle in the oil until emulsified. Alternatively, place all the ingredients in a glass jar or bottle and shake vigorously until well mixed.

NOTE: Use this as a base and flavour with finely chopped fresh herbs, tomatoes (seeds removed), capers, dried herbs and spices, or chilli flakes.

Chilli Vinaigrette

MAKES ½ CUP

110 g (½ cup) sugar
125 ml (½ cup) white vinegar
1-2 red chillies, finely chopped, to taste
1 strip of lemon rind
1 kaffir lime leaf
1 clove garlic, crushed

Bring to the boil the sugar and white vinegar. Add the chopped red chilli, lemon rind, kaffir lime leaf and crushed garlic. Reduce until syrupy. Note that as it cools, the liquid will thicken up.

NOTE: This vinaigrette keeps well in a sterilised glass jar so you can make a larger batch. Feel free to adjust the flavours to your liking.

Hot and Sour Dressing

MAKES ⅓ CUP

3 teaspoons freshly squeezed
  lime juice
1 teaspoon fish sauce
1 teaspoon sweet chilli sauce
½ teaspoon finely chopped
  garlic
½ teaspoon finely chopped hot
  red chilli
1 teaspoon finely chopped
  coriander stems

Whisk all ingredients together until well combined.

Citrus Tamari or Soy Dressing

MAKES 1 CUP

1 large sweet orange, zest and
  juice (should yield about 100 ml,
  about ½ cup, juice)
3⅓ tablespoons tamari or premium
  soy sauce
⅔ tablespoon good quality dark
  soy sauce (exclude this for a
  gluten-free version)
3⅓ tablespoons brown rice vinegar
4 shallots, peeled, thinly sliced
1 tablespoon brown sugar
1 teaspoon sesame oil

Whisk all ingredients together until well combined.

Sesame and Soy Dressing

MAKES ⅓ CUP

2½ tablespoons soy sauce
2 tablespoons brown rice vinegar
3 teaspoons sesame oil
4 teaspoons sweet chilli sauce
2½ tablespoons light olive oil (or
  vegetable oil)

Whisk all ingredients together until well combined.

*Clockwise from left: Sesame and Soy
Dressing (page 169), Hot and Sour
Dressing, Citrus Soy Dressing (both above)
and Basic Vinaigrette (page 169).*

Special, Sweet Stuff

Desserts are my Achilles heel! I absolutely love them, particularly cakes, cookies and tarts with lots of fruits – fresh or dried – and where there is a good balance of fruitiness, sweetness and tartness.

I tend to bake with much less sugar and prefer desserts that aren't too rich or sickly sweet. You'll never really find traditional icing in any of the cakes I make but rather, freshly whipped cream or cream cheese icing that has a touch of sweetness but always with an addition of vanilla or citrus zest!

Living in Australia, I have been spoilt with the choice of seasonal fruit. It's so important to learn about the different varieties of fruit and which to use for your desserts, and what adjustments are needed to be made as it makes a big difference in the way the cake or pastry turns out.

Rich Lemon Butter Cake
with Brandied Prunes

SERVES 12-16

Mom has been making her butter cake for the family since I was little. I remember the wafts of cake-baking aroma coming from her kitchen, a teaser for what was about to come. I could never wait for the cake to cool completely before cutting myself a slice!

I have happy memories of having cake and tea sessions with Mom and Dad, just enjoying the simple delights that she created from her kitchen.

As this cake is made with lots of butter, it's much nicer for summer as the warm weather keeps the cake lovely and moist.

125 g (4.4 oz) dried prunes
2 tablespoons brandy, whisky (Jamieson) or dark rum
200 g (1⅓ cups) plain flour
1 teaspoon baking powder
225 g (8 oz) salted butter, room temperature
180 g (6.5 oz) caster sugar
4 eggs
2 lemons, zest
1 tablespoon lemon juice

Soak the prunes in the brandy, whisky or rum overnight.

Preheat your oven to 180°C (356°F).

Butter and line the base of a 20 x 10 x 6 cm (8 x 4 x 2.5 inch) loaf tin or 20 cm (8 in) round or square cake tin with greaseproof paper.

Sift together the flour and baking powder in a mixing bowl.

In an electric mixer, cream the butter and sugar until pale and fluffy. Add the eggs one at a time, beating well after each addition. Beat in the lemon zest. Add the flour and pulse until almost combined then add the juice. Pulse until just combined.

Gently fold in the prunes and any remaining soaking liquor. Pour into the loaf or cake tin and bake for 45-50 minutes or until a skewer inserted into the thickest part of the cake comes out clean.

Cool on a wire rack for 10 minutes before turning out. Cool completely or serve slightly warm.

NOTE: The prunes are optional. If you choose not to soak the prunes, simply stud it through the cake mix in the tin before baking.

I use normal salted butter for this cake and ensure that the butter is at room temperature.

Coconut and Banana Bread
with Gula Melaka Almond Crunch

SERVES 8-10

This brings together my love for banana bread, coconut milk and gula melaka (coconut sugar). They work so well together and, trust me, it's so delectable that a single slice just isn't enough. You'll be coming back for more. Whenever I make this, the kids always want a slice in their lunch box. For me, lightly toasted, smothered with good butter and a cup of tea will do.

300 g (2 cups) self-raising flour, sifted

260 g (just over 1 cup) caster sugar

Pinch of salt

135 g (1¾ cups) shredded dried coconut

400 ml (1⅔ cups) coconut milk

2 eggs

2 teaspoons vanilla extract

4 small, ripe but not mushy bananas, thickly sliced

TOPPING

20 g (0.7 oz) gula melaka (coconut sugar), shaved

20 g (0.7 oz) slivered almonds

Preheat your oven to 180°C (356°F). Butter and line the base and sides of a loaf tin 31 cm x 11 cm x 7.5 cm (2 lb capacity) with greaseproof paper.

Mix together the flour, sugar and salt in a large mixing bowl using a whisk. Toss in the shredded coconut and mix well.

In a separate bowl, whisk together the coconut milk, eggs and vanilla. Add to the flour mixture and fold until just combined. Fold in the sliced bananas and be careful not to break them up.

Pour into the loaf tin and top with the gula melaka shavings and almonds.

Bake for 1½ hours or until the top is golden and a skewer inserted into the thickest part of the loaf comes out clean.

Cool in the tin for 10 minutes, then turn out onto a rack. Cool completely or serve slightly warm.

Baked Apricot and Rosemary Tart

SERVES 8-10

The flavour of fresh apricots really intensifies after being baked. The amount of sugar you add will largely depend on the season's crop. If they are quite sweet, reduce the amount of sugar used. The rosemary and vanilla enhances the flavour of the apricots and make a difference. I love it! These baked apricots are also great with yoghurt and muesli, or your favourite vanilla bean ice cream.

500 g (1.1 lbs) fresh apricots
2-4 sprigs fresh rosemary
2 vanilla beans, halved
   lengthways, seeds scraped
Raw sugar to taste

PASTRY
170 g (6 oz) plain flour
Pinch of salt
85 g (3 oz) cold unsalted butter,
   cubed
2-3 tablespoons ice water with a
   dash of white vinegar

Preheat the oven to 200°C (392°F). Butter and lightly dust a 24 cm (9.5 in) round, loose-base tart tin or four 10 cm (4 in) loose-base tart tins.

Halve the apricots and remove the seeds. Lay the apricot halves on a baking pan lined with greaseproof paper, scatter over the top the rosemary, vanilla and sugar. Bake for 20-30 minutes or until the sugar has dissolved and apricots have softened but still retaining its shape. Remove from the oven and set aside to cool.

To make the pastry, place the flour and salt in a food processor and blitz for 10 seconds. Add the butter and pulse until the mixture resembles breadcrumbs. With the motor running, add just enough water to form a dough. Empty onto a clean surface, gently pat together to form a flat disc, wrap with cling film and refrigerate for 20-30 minutes.

Roll the dough out between two plastic sheets or baking paper to 2 mm (about 0.1 in) thickness, making frequent quarter turns to create a round shape. Line the tart tin with the pastry, tucking well into the corners. Trim the edges neatly. Line with greaseproof paper or foil and fill with uncooked rice or baking beads and blind bake for 20-25 minutes or until the edges are crisp. Remove the rice and paper and bake for a further 5-10 minutes until the pastry is cooked through, golden and crisp. Remove from the oven and set aside to cool.

Lay the apricots generously over the base of the tart shell. Top with my Vanilla Pastry Cream (see note on page 202) and drizzle with the remaining syrup.

Moist Carrot Cake with
Toasted Walnuts and Golden Raisins

SERVES 8-12

I have so many favourite cakes but a good carrot cake ranks quite highly on my list. The best ones I've tasted were definitely in New Zealand. Hot chocolate and carrot cake were a common choice at cafes there. Hopefully, this recipe will satisfy all your sweet, carrot cravings!

300 g (2 cups) plain flour
1 teaspoon baking soda
½ teaspoon baking powder
2 teaspoons ground cinnamon
½ teaspoon ground allspice
¼ teaspoon ground cloves
½ cup toasted walnuts
½ cup golden raisins
250 ml (1 cup) oil
220 g (1 cup) fine or soft brown
    sugar
3 eggs
1½ teaspoons vanilla extract
300 g (2 cups) firmly packed
    grated carrot

CREAM CHEESE ICING
250 g (1 cup) cream cheese
1 heaped tablespoon icing sugar
1 orange, zest
125 ml (½ cup) thickened cream,
    whisked to stiff peaks

Preheat your oven to 180°C (356°F). Butter and line a 23 x 13 x 7 cm (2 lb capacity) loaf tin with greaseproof paper.

Sift all the dry ingredients together. Toss the nuts and raisins into the flour.

In a separate mixing bowl, whisk together the oil, sugar and eggs until well combined. Add in the vanilla and beat well. Fold in the flour, nuts and raisins until almost combined, then mix in the grated carrots.

Pour into the loaf tin and bake for 45-50 minutes or until a fine skewer inserted into the thickest part of the cake comes out clean.

Remove from the oven, cool for 10 minutes, then turn out onto a rack to cool completely.

To make the cream cheese icing, whisk together the cream cheese, icing sugar and orange zest until smooth.

Whisk the thickened cream separately. Add half of the whipped thickened cream into the cream cheese mixture and whisk until smooth, then fold in the remainder.

Serve the cake with dollops of cream cheese icing over the top!

NOTE: It is important to use fine or soft brown sugar in this recipe. This will allow the oil and sugar to emulsify well.

Mom's Apple Pie

SERVES 8-12

Ask me where I've had the best apple pies and I will tell you only in my mother's kitchen. She makes her filling sweet and tart and buttery. As much as the filling is important, the pastry needs to be spot on, short and crumbly. This is the only apple pie I make now and often include peaches or berries depending on what's in season.

PASTRY

300 g (2 cups) plain flour
Pinch of salt
240 g (8.5 oz) cold unsalted
    butter, cubed
3 tablespoons ice water with a
    dash of white vinegar

FILLING

5 large apples (Granny Smith,
    Gala or Pink Lady), peeled and
    cored
100 g (3.5 oz) plump raisins or
    sultanas
1 large orange, zest and juice
$\frac{1}{2}$ lemon, zest and juice (optional)
3 tablespoons raw sugar
$\frac{1}{2}$-1 teaspoon ground
    cinnamon, or to taste
2 tablespoons plain flour
25 g (0.9 oz) extra unsalted
    butter

1 egg, lightly beaten for egg wash

Preheat your oven to 180°C (356°F). Lightly butter a 20 cm (8 in) loose-base pie dish or a 30 cm (12 in) flan dish.

To prepare the filling, halve the apples and slice thinly (1 mm, .04 in). Mix all the filling ingredients together except for the extra butter in a large bowl and set aside.

To make the pastry, place the flour and salt in a food processor and blitz for 10 seconds. Add the butter and pulse until the mixture resembles breadcrumbs. With the motor running, add just enough water to form a dough. Empty onto a clean surface, gently pat to form a flat disc, wrap with cling film and refrigerate for 20-30 minutes.

Divide the pastry into two equal portions. Roll each between two plastic sheets or baking paper to 2 mm (.08 in) thickness, making frequent quarter turns to create a round shape. Line the pie dish with one pastry sheet, trimming the edges with a knife. Line with greaseproof paper and fill with uncooked rice or baking beads, then blind bake for 20-25 minutes or until the edges are lightly golden. Remove the rice and paper and bake for a further 5 minutes. Remove from the oven and cool completely.

Fill the cooked pastry evenly with the apple mixture. Place small knobs of the extra butter evenly over the top of the fruit. Cover with the remaining raw pastry sheet, moulding well over the fruit towards the edges. Pinch the edges of the pie to seal. Brush with egg wash.

Poke a large hole about 1 cm (0.4 in) wide in the middle of the pie and 3-4 smaller holes around the top with a chopstick and bake for 1 hour or until nicely golden and you can see the juices bubbling through the holes.

Remove from the oven, rest for 15 minutes, then serve with my homemade Runny Vanilla Custard (page 203) or your favourite vanilla bean ice cream.

Note: In warmer climates, you may not require as much water for the dough to come together. If the dough is too difficult to manage, roll the pastry out and leave it in the fridge to firm up.

Apple and Berry Walnut Crumble
SERVES 8-10

Apple, berries, citrus, golden crumble.... I think you've guessed the type of desserts I love. I am indeed simple when it comes to my favourite things to eat! This is simply perfect for all occasions.

Like the apple pie, use Gala or Pink Lady apples. This recipe uses frozen berries which will leach out extra liquid. Use less flour if you are using fresh berries.

FILLING

4 large apples (Gala or Pink Lady), peeled and cored
1 orange, zest and juice (yielding about 80 ml, ⅓ cup)
50 g (⅓ cup) raisins
75 g (½ cup) frozen mixed berries
3-4 tablespoons raw sugar
½ teaspoon ground cinnamon
3 tablespoons plain flour
25 g (0.9 oz) butter

CRUMBLE

75 g (½ cup) plain flour
50 g (½ cup) rolled oats
55 g (¼ cup) firmly packed brown sugar
¾ teaspoon ground cinnamon
75 g (2.5 oz) walnuts, lightly toasted
75 g (2.5 oz) cold butter, cubed

Preheat your oven to 180°C (356°F). Lightly butter the sides of a 15 cm x 20 cm (6 in x 8 in) ovenproof casserole dish, or 8-10 ramekins.

To make the filling, cut the apples into half and slice thinly (1 mm, .04 in). Mix together all the ingredients except for the butter and toss to combine. Set aside.

To make the crumble, place all the ingredients in a food processor and pulse until coarse and lumpy crumbs are formed.

Place the filling in the casserole dish and top with little blobs of the butter evenly over the top. Then cover evenly with the crumbs.

Bake for 50-55 minutes until the apples are tender and the crumble is golden. Serve with your favourite vanilla bean ice cream or my Runny Vanilla Custard (page 203).

NOTE: If you like more crumble, increase the quantities of the ingredients in the same proportion. Try combinations of other fillings such as peaches and nectarines.

Salted Caramel Chocolate Tarts

MAKES 4-6 SMALL TARTS OR 1 LARGE TART

Desserts go in and out of fashion. This tart, however, will never go out of fashion in my book. The combination of dark, almost burnt caramel with a hint of pink salt, a swirl of chocolate and a light crisp decadent chocolate short crust pastry makes my mouth water just thinking about it. I'm fairly certain that you will have a tablespoon of caramel even before you start putting the tart together! Then again, I can't guarantee you'll stop at just one! It is incredibly addictive and so delicious.

I take the caramel quite far on the stove so it's dark and not at all too sweet, just the way I like it. If you prefer, add a little more cream. I find these a little easier to serve in small individual tarts than a large tart, but both will work fine. As a sinful gesture, make a jar of caramel and drizzle it over good vanilla ice cream.

CHOCOLATE PASTRY

170 g (6 oz) plain flour
Pinch of salt
2 heaped tablespoons cocoa
  powder
2 levelled tablespoons icing sugar
130 g (4.5 oz) cold unsalted
  butter, cubed
2-3 tablespoons ice water with a
  dash of white vinegar

Preheat your oven to 180°C (356°F). Butter and lightly flour four 10 cm (4 in) loose-base, fluted tart tins or 1 large, loose-base tart tin.

To make the pastry, place the flour, salt, cocoa, and sugar in a food processor and blitz for 30 seconds until well combined. Add the butter and pulse until the mixture resembles breadcrumbs. With the motor running, add just enough water until the dough comes together. Empty onto a clean surface, gently pat together to form a flat disc, wrap with cling film and refrigerate for 20-30 minutes.

Roll the pastry between two clean plastic sheets to 2 mm (.08 in) thick. Line each tart tin with pastry, trimming the edge to fit the tin. Refrigerate until the pastry is firm. Line the tarts with greaseproof paper and uncooked rice or baking beads, and bake for 15-20 minutes until firm around the edges. Remove the beads and paper, and bake for further 5-10 minutes or until pastry is cooked through and crisp to the touch. Remove from the oven and set aside to cool.

Make the salted caramel (page 188).

Pour the cooled caramel into the crispy tart shells. Drop a spoonful of melted dark chocolate, then use a wooden skewer to create swirls. Sprinkle over some pink salt and serve with vanilla cream.

Salted Caramel

MAKES ABOUT 1 CUP

100 g (½ cup) soft light brown
   sugar
100 g (½ cup) caster sugar
100 ml (⅓ cup plus 2 tablespoons)
   thickened or double cream
1 teaspoon sea salt or pink salt
100 g (3.5 oz) unsalted butter,
   room temperature

Measure all the ingredients and place on the bench top. Place a bowl of water and a pastry brush (unfortunately you can't use the silicon ones for this) nearby. You may need to brush around the frying pan just above the sugar to avoid crystals from forming..

Sprinkle the caster sugar evenly onto a medium frying pan and place over medium heat. When the sugar starts melting around the edges, swirl the pan around to incorporate the rest of the sugar. As soon as the sugar has melted, sprinkle over the brown sugar in one or two batches. Swirl to combine. This might take a little while and your undivided attention, so be patient!

Scald the cream separately. As soon as all the sugar has dissolved and the caramel has turned a deep golden colour, remove from the heat immediately and pour in the cream, whisking continuously. Be careful, as it will hiss quite a bit. Finally, add the salt and butter and whisk until smooth and glossy. Set aside to cool.

NOTE: Once the sugar starts to turn golden, watch it like a hawk as the change will happen very quickly and it is easy to burn your caramel resulting in a very bitter, inedible finish.

When the sugar crystallises, there is little you can do to salvage it. So gentle brushing of the pan just above the melted sugar with a damp brush will help avoid this.

Chocolate Frangipane Tart with Poached Pears

SERVES 8-10

Frangipane tarts are delicious and everyone should learn to make them. Use good quality vanilla extract and the yummiest fruit for the best results. There are a number of fruits that work really well with a frangipane: Pear, figs, dark sweet plums, just to name a few. The wonderful thing about this tart is you can bake it with the fruit or add the fruit after baking. You can also add chocolate to the frangipane mix to create another dessert altogether. It is by far, truly, my favourite tart!

PASTRY

170 g (6 oz) plain flour
Pinch of salt
4 levelled tablespoons cocoa
  powder
2 levelled tablespoons icing sugar
130 g (4.5 oz) cold unsalted
  butter, cubed
1 egg yolk

CHOCOLATE FRANGIPANE

100 g (3.5 oz) unsalted butter,
  softened at room temperature
100 g (3.5 oz) caster sugar, sifted
2 eggs
1 vanilla bean, halved
  lengthways, seeds scraped
170 g (6 oz) dark chocolate,
  melted and cooled
100 g (3.5 oz) almond meal
1 tablespoon flour

Preheat oven to 180°C (356°F). Butter and lightly dust with flour a 24 cm (9.5-in) loose-base fluted tart tin.

To make the pastry, place the flour, salt, cocoa, and sugar in a food processor and blitz for 30 seconds until well combined. Add the butter and pulse until the mixture resembles breadcrumbs. With the motor running, add the egg yolk and process until dough comes together. Empty onto a clean surface, gently pat together to form a flat disc, wrap with cling film and refrigerate for 20-30 minutes.

Prepare the poached pears (page 192).

Roll the pastry out between two clean plastic sheets to 2 mm (about 0.1 in) thickness. Line the tart tin with the pastry, tucking well into the corners. Trim the edges neatly. Line with greaseproof paper or foil and fill with uncooked rice or baking beads and blind bake for 20-25 minutes or until the edges are crisp. Remove the rice and paper, and bake for a further 5 minutes. Remove from the oven and set aside to cool.

For the chocolate frangipane, cream the butter and sugar together until pale and fluffy. Add the eggs one at a time, beating well after each addition. Beat in the vanilla. Add the melted chocolate and beat until well mixed, then fold in the almond meal and flour.

Fill the tart shell with the frangipane, smooth the surface and bake for 25-30 minutes or until frangipane is cooked. Remove from the oven and set aside to cool.

When it has completely cooled, carefully remove the tart from the tins and place onto a serving dish.

I like to halve some pears and leave some whole. Place them around the tart. Drizzle the tart with a little poaching syrup and serve with my Vanilla Bean Cream (page 202).

Fig, Pistachio and Honey Frangipane Tart

SERVES 8-10

4 fresh figs
1-2 tablespoons honey
1 tablespoon toasted pistachio
  kernels, crushed to coarse
  crumbs

PASTRY
170 g (6 oz) plain flour
Pinch of salt
85 g (3 oz) cold unsalted butter,
  cubed
2-3 tablespoons ice water with a
  dash of white vinegar

FRANGIPANE
100 g (3.5 oz) unsalted butter,
  softened at room temperature
100 g (3.5 oz) caster sugar, sifted
2 eggs
1 teaspoon vanilla extract or
  1 vanilla bean, halved
  lengthways, seeds scraped
100 g (3.5 oz) almond meal
1 tablespoon flour

Preheat your oven to 180°C (356°F). Butter and lightly dust with flour a round 24 cm (9.5 in) loose-base tart tin or a 35 x 13 x 2.5 cm (44 x 4.75 x 1 in) rectangular loose-base tart tin.

To make the pastry, place the flour and salt in a food processor and blitz for 30 seconds until well combined. Add the butter and pulse until the mixture resembles breadcrumbs. With the motor running, add just enough water for dough to come together. Empty onto a clean surface, gently pat together to form a flat disc, wrap with cling film and refrigerate for 20-30 minutes.

Roll the pastry out between two clean plastic sheets to 2 mm (about 0.1 in) thickness. Line the tart tin with the pastry, tucking well into the corners. Trim the edges neatly. Line with greaseproof paper or foil and fill with uncooked rice or baking beads and blind bake for 20-25 minutes or until the edges are slightly golden. Remove the rice and paper and bake for a further 5 minutes. Remove from the oven and set aside to cool.

For the frangipane, cream the butter and sugar together until pale and fluffy. Add the eggs one at a time, beating well after each addition. Beat in the vanilla. Fold in the almond meal and flour.

Fill the cooled tart shell with the frangipane, smooth out the surface and bake for 25-30 minutes or until the frangipane is cooked and golden. Remove from the oven and allow to cool until just warm.

Halve three figs and leave one whole. Haphazardly place them on top of the tart, drizzle with honey and sprinkle with pistachios crumbs.

Serve with my Vanilla Bean Cream (page 202).

NOTE: For the pistachio crumbs, toast a tablespoon of pistachio kernels (without their shells) in the oven at 180°C (356°F) for 5-10 minutes. Allow to cool, then grind in a mortar and pestle to a coarse crumb.

Pear and Honey Frangipane Tart

2 large ripe Packham or
  Bosc pears
1-2 tablespoons honey

For a pear and honey version of a frangipane tart (see page 190), prepare the pears by peeling the skin, core, halve and slice thinly into ½ cm (0.2 in) thick wedges.

Fill the tart shell with the frangipane, then top with the sliced pears in a circular design. Bake for 35 to 40 minutes until lightly golden. Remove from the oven and immediately drizzle over the honey.

Poached Pears in Vincotto and Vanilla Beans

SERVES 6

I absolutely love poached pears! Add the Vincotto and vanilla bean and it's just divine! These make a fabulous topping for tarts and are brilliant with your favourite toasted muesli and yoghurt for a snazzy breakie. If you're a purist, then just serve them as they are, drizzled with the reduced poaching liquor along with your favourite vanilla bean ice cream. A very sophisticated dessert for a dinner party!

5 medium ripe firm pears (Bosc,
  Packham), peeled
500 ml (2 cups) water
220 g (1 cup) caster sugar
1 vanilla bean, halved
  lengthways, seeds scraped
1 lemon, zest and juice
80 ml (⅓ cup) Vincotto

Place all the ingredients except the pears in a saucepan large enough to fit all the pears snuggly. Bring to a boil and cook for 2 minutes until all the sugar has dissolved. Place the pears in the saucepan, cover with a sheet of greaseproof paper made into a cartouche.

As soon as the liquid comes up to the boil again, lower the heat and simmer until the pears are tender. To check, run a small and thin sharp knife through the thickest part of the pear and there should be little resistance.

To reduce the poaching liquor, remove all the pears and boil until the liquor is reduced to your liking.

NOTE: Vincotto is made by slow cooking and reducing non-fermented dark grape juice to a delicious syrup that is then cellared to develop their own unique flavour profile. If you are unable to find Vincotto, add a touch of balsamic glaze or omit.

A cartouche is made from greaseproof paper. Here, it acts as a lid to slow down the reduction of moisture when poaching. To make a cartouche, take a square piece of greaseproof paper, fold into a triangle, then fold into half again on the folded end, and then once again. To measure the size, hold the tip in the middle of the saucepan, then cut around the edge of the pan.

Cinnamon, Apple and Walnut Bundt Cake

SERVES 16

Apples, cinnamon, nutmeg and cloves are a fabulous combination. Top this with a walnut praline and you will be guaranteed to be transported to a very happy place!

This cake is made with oil instead of butter, so it is incredibly soft and moist. It's the sort of cake that is perfect for winter when apples are in season in Australia. There is nothing better than a spiced apple cake with a strong cup of Orange Pekoe tea to satisfy any cake craving!

4 medium apples (Pink Lady or Gala apples are perfect), peeled, cored and coarsely grated using a box grater into a basin placed at an angle to drain slightly

300 g (2 cups) plain flour

1 teaspoon bicarbonate of soda

180 g ($^4/_5$ cup) caster sugar

1 teaspoon salt

1 teaspoon ground cinnamon

$^1/_2$ teaspoon ground nutmeg

$^1/_4$ teaspoon ground cloves

100 g (3.5 oz) crimson raisins or raisins or sultanas

3 eggs

250 ml (1 cup) oil (light olive oil, rice bran or vegetable oil)

1$^1/_2$ teaspoon vanilla extract

WALNUT PRALINE

200 g (a little less than 1 cup) caster sugar

50 g ($^1/_2$ cup) toasted walnuts

Preheat your oven to 180°C (356°F). Butter and lightly flour a 10-cup capacity bundt tin. If you don't have a bundt tin, use a 20 cm (8 in) round or square cake tin.

Sift together the flour, bicarbonate of soda, sugar, salt and spices in a large mixing bowl. Use a whisk to mix them together. Alternatively, blitz this in a food processor. Add in the crimson raisins and toss to combine.

In a separate mixing bowl, whisk together the eggs, oil and vanilla until well combined. Add in the flour mixture and gently fold until just combined. Add in the apples and mix to combine. It will seem like there is a lot of apple for the mixture, so be careful and don't be tempted to over mix.

Pour into the bundt tin, level the top and bake for 50-55 minutes or till a fine skewer inserted in the thickest part of the cake comes out clean. Cool on a wire rack for 10 minutes before turning the cake out.

To make the praline, line a baking sheet with greaseproof paper. Prepare a bowl of water and place a pastry brush nearby. Start by heating a clean frying pan over medium heat. Add enough sugar to thinly cover the surface of the pan. Once the sugar starts to melt around the edges, swirl the pan around to mix with the rest of the sugar. When most or all of the sugar has melted, sprinkle more sugar into the pan. Repeat until all the sugar has melted. At this stage, pay close attention as the caramel will turn very quickly. You want to cook it to a dark golden brown colour but not burn the caramel. Sprinkle in the toasted walnuts, quickly toss and pour out onto the lined baking sheet. Leave to cool completely. Once it cools, the praline will harden. Break into pieces and roughly grind in a chopper or food processor.

Sift some icing sugar on the cake, sprinkle with the walnut praline and serve with freshly-whipped Vanilla Bean Cream (page 202).

Rich Chocolate Beetroot Cake

SERVES 10-12

Beetroot and chocolate are a perfect match. Both have the same earthiness which results in a rich but mellow cake. While I'm not obsessed with chocolate, I do like a rich moist dark chocolate cake with no added frills. The beetroot helps to keep the cake really moist. This can be made into little cupcakes, or if you can get hold of a shallow cake tin that has beautiful designs, it will look really lovely when you turn the cake out. Note that this cake will rise quite a bit while it's baking and drop back after.

150 g (1 cup) plain flour
165 g (¾ cup) caster sugar
40 g (⅓ cup) cocoa powder
¾ teaspoon bicarbonate of soda
¼ teaspoon baking powder
100 g (1 cup) beetroot, peeled, grated
60 ml (¼ cup) oil
250 g (1 cup) sour cream or plain yoghurt
1 egg
1½ teaspoons vanilla extract
150 g (4.7 oz) 70% dark chocolate, finely chopped

CHOCOLATE GANACHE
200 g (7 oz) dark chocolate
125 ml (½ cup) cream

Preheat your oven to 170°C (338°F). Butter and line the base of a 20 cm (8 in) shallow round cake tin or a cupcake tin with greaseproof paper.

In a food processor, blitz together the flour, sugar, cocoa powder, bicarbonate of soda and baking powder. Add the grated beetroot, oil, sour cream, egg and vanilla and process for 2 minutes, scraping down the sides a couple of times. Include the chocolate and pulse until well combined.

Pour into your prepared cake tin and bake for 50-55 minutes or until a skewer inserted in the thickest part of the cake comes out clean. Cupcakes will take 35-40 minutes to cook.

Rest the cake in the tin for 5 minutes, then turn over onto a rack to cool completely.

To make the chocolate ganache, place the dark chocolate in a mixing bowl. Bring the cream to the boil, then immediately remove and pour over the chocolate. Stir until all the chocolate has melted and the mixture is smooth and shiny.

To serve, drizzle over the chocolate ganache and have a dollop of freshly whipped Vanilla Bean Cream (page 202) on the side.

Orange Chiffon Cake

SERVES 20

This was my staple growing up. It has my childhood written all over it. Mom would always use a tablespoon or so of Sunkist orange concentrate. Any leftovers after a few days would be turned into a trifle with orange custard and canned peaches. So retro but just sensational!

5 egg yolks
200 g (1 cup) caster sugar
125 ml (½ cup) oil
2-3 oranges, zest
250 ml (1 cup) freshly squeezed
orange juice
300 g (2 cups) plain flour, sifted
2 teaspoons baking powder
6 egg whites
½ teaspoon cream of tartar

Preheat oven to 180°C (356°F). Set aside a 25 cm (10 in) chiffon cake tin.

In a large mixing bowl, whisk together the egg yolks, 150 g (¾ cup) of sugar, oil, orange zest and juice until smooth. In a separate bowl, mix together the flour and baking powder. Add the flour to the batter and whisk until smooth.

Whisk the egg whites and cream of tartar in an electric mixer until foamy. Gradually add the rest of the sugar and whisk until stiff peaks. Add a third of the whisked whites to the cake batter and whisk till smooth. Add the remaining whisked whites and gently fold until just combined. To maintain a light cake, be careful not to over mix.

Pour the batter into the cake tin and bake for 50-55 minutes. Remove from the oven and immediately turn the cake tin upside down to cool. I find using a large funnel placed upside down on a flat surface is best for this. When the cake has cooled completely, use a sharp, thin knife to separate the cake from the tin by running it around the sides, at the base and around the middle before turning out.

Slice and serve with my Orange Citrus Cream (page 201).

NOTE: It is important to note that when making chiffon cakes, the cake tins are not buttered. This allows the cake to be turned over to cool.

Moist Orange Cake with Orange Citrus Cream

SERVES 16

Anything with orange zest in it ranks highly on my list of "likes". Cakes, in particular, perfumed with the zest of oranges are fresh and just divine. This is an adaption of a recipe a friend gave me years ago and I will continue to bake it for years to come.

280 g (1⅓ cups) caster sugar

280 g (1 cup) natural or Greek yoghurt

250 ml (1 cup) oil (light olive, rice bran or vegetable)

2 eggs

2 oranges, zest

300 g (2 cups) self-raising flour

1 tablespoon orange juice

1 tablespoon lemon juice

Preheat your oven to 180°C (356°F). Butter and line the base of a 20 cm (8 in) round cake tin with greaseproof paper. Dust lightly with flour.

In a large mixing bowl, whisk together the sugar, yoghurt, oil, eggs and zest until smooth. Sift in the flour and fold through. The batter should appear lumpy with blobs of flour. Pour the juices around the edges of the cake batter and fold through, taking care not to over mix.

Pour straight into your prepared cake tin and bake for 50 minutes to an hour or until a fine skewer inserted in the thickest part of the cake comes out clean. Remove from the oven and cool for 10 minutes before turning out onto a wire rack. Leave to cool completely.

Ice the cake with the Orange Citrus Cream (see below) only when it has cooled completely. Create a smooth or swirly finish.

Orange Citrus Cream

MAKES 2½ CUPS

300 ml (1⅕ cups) thickened cream

2 heaped tablespoons icing sugar, sifted

1 orange, zest

Whisk together the cream, icing sugar and orange zest until soft but firm peaks. Keep refrigerated until ready to use.

Vanilla Bean Cream

300 ml (1⅕ cup) thickened cream
2 tablespoons icing sugar
1 teaspoon of vanilla extract or
   1 vanilla bean, split lengthwise,
   seeds scraped

Whisk the thickened cream, icing sugar and vanilla extract or seeds of vanilla bean until soft peaks. Do not over whisk or your cream will be lumpy and separate. In warmer climates, ensure the cream is kept cool and preferably work in a cool room.

Coconut and Pandan Pastry Cream

MAKES 1½ -2 CUPS

Pastry cream is possibly the single most delicious sweet thing on my list of favourite desserts. It is very versatile and can be used with cakes, pastries or tarts. This is my coconut and pandan version, a beautiful accompaniment to my Coconut Pandan Chiffon Cake (page 204).

400 ml (1⅔ cups) coconut milk
80 g (⅓ cup) caster sugar
3 levelled tablespoons cornflour
4 egg yolks
1-2 teaspoon pandan extract
200 ml (⅘ cup) thickened cream,
   whisked till soft peaks

In a medium saucepan, bring the coconut milk to a boil, then immediately remove from heat and set aside.

Whisk together the sugar, cornflour, egg yolks and pandan extract in a large mixing bowl until pale and creamy. Gradually whisk in all the hot coconut milk.

Return the mixture into the saucepan and whisk over medium heat until the mixture thickens. Remove from the heat and pour into a glass bowl, cover with cling film directly on top of the mixture to avoid a skin from forming and refrigerate to cool.

Once the mixture is cool, stir it up with a wooden spoon until smooth. In a separate bowl, whisk the thickened cream until soft peaks. Fold the cream into the custard, starting with a couple of tablespoons to loosen the mixture, followed by the rest. Refrigerate until ready to use.

NOTE: For a Vanilla Pastry Cream, replace the coconut milk with full cream milk and the pandan extract with 1-1½ teaspoons vanilla extract or paste, or 1 vanilla bean, seeds scraped.

Runny Vanilla Custard

MAKES 2 CUPS

No one can resist a good custard in my family. Forget the store-bought stuff; make your own and you'll never look back. Drizzle it over a pie, Christmas pudding, tarts or – if you dare – pour it into a cup and simply enjoy with a big spoon!

200 ml (⁴/₅ cup) milk
200 ml (⁴/₅ cup) thickened cream
1 vanilla bean, split lengthwise
   and seeds scraped, or 1¹/₂
   teaspoons vanilla extract
3 egg yolks
2 heaped tablespoons caster
   sugar, or to taste

In a medium saucepan, heat the milk, thickened cream, vanilla seeds and pod until it just starts to boil. Remove from the heat immediately and set aside.

Whisk the egg yolks and sugar in a mixing bowl until pale and fluffy. Gradually whisk in the hot milk and cream mixture through a sieve.

Return the mixture into the saucepan, cook on low heat, stirring with a wooden spoon until the mixture coats the back of the spoon. A good way to test this is to run your finger over the spoon. The line should remain intact. Remove from heat immediately and set aside to cool. Be careful not to overcook this or the custard will curdle.

NOTE: For a slightly thicker custard, whisk in 2 teaspoons of cornflour with the egg yolks and sugar. Invest in good vanilla extract, paste or beans (not essence!) particularly if it's going into a simple dish like ice cream or custard. It's worth the while!

Coconut Pandan Chiffon Cake

SERVES 20

Chiffon cakes are such Seventies and Eighties cakes. However, I think they are the perfect cake, a little more moist and flavoursome compared to sponges. Mom made the best chiffon cakes. Growing up, I would watch her make them step by step and often got a turn to whisk the yolks and juice mixture. This is my coconut and pandan version.

5 egg yolks
200 g (1 cup) caster sugar
125 ml (½ cup) oil
250 ml (1 cup) coconut milk
1½ teaspoons pandan extract
300 g (2 cups) plain flour, sifted
2 teaspoons baking powder
6 egg whites
½ teaspoon cream of tartar

Preheat your oven to 180°C (356°F). Set aside a 25 cm (10 in) chiffon cake tin.

In a large mixing bowl, whisk together the egg yolks, 150 g (¾ cup) of sugar, oil, coconut milk and pandan extract until smooth. In a separate bowl, sift together the flour and baking powder.

Whisk egg whites and cream of tartar in an electric mixer until foamy. Gradually add the rest of the sugar and whisk until stiff peaks. Add a third of the whisked whites to the cake batter and whisk until smooth. Add the remaining whisked whites and gently fold until just combined. To maintain a light cake, be careful not to over mix.

Pour the batter into the prepared cake tin and bake for 50-55 minutes.

Remove from the oven and immediately turn the cake tin upside down to cool. I find using a large funnel placed upside down on a flat surface is best for this. When the cake has cooled completely, use a sharp, thin knife to separate the cake from the tin by running it around the sides, at the base and around the middle before turning out.

Slice and serve with my Coconut and Pandan Pastry Cream (page 202).

NOTE: It is important to note that when making chiffon cakes, the cake tins are not greased. This allows the cake to be turned over to cool. This is what creates the light, airy nature of this cake.

Sticky Rum, Fig and Honey Ice Cream

MAKES ABOUT 1 LITRE

If you've never made ice-cream, you have to give it a go. There is nothing like using the freshest eggs, milk and cream and churning your own. The bonus is that you get to add any flavourings you like. Here is a combo that combines two of my favourite ingredients – figs and honey!

250 ml (1 cup) milk
250 ml (1 cup) thickened cream
1 vanilla bean, seeds scraped
120 ml (a little over ⅓ cup) honey
4 egg yolks
100 g (3.5 oz) rum-poached
    dried figs (see note below)

Prepare a large basin of ice water.

Place the milk, thickened cream and vanilla bean (bean and seeds) in a saucepan, bring to the boil and remove from the heat.

In the meantime, whisk the honey and egg yolks together in a mixing bowl until light and pale. Slowly whisk in the hot milk and cream mixture through a sieve to catch the vanilla bean.

Return the mixture to the saucepan, cook on low heat, stirring with a wooden spoon until the mixture coats the back of the wooden spoon. A good way to test this is to run your finger over the spoon. The line should remain intact. Be careful not to overcook this or the custard will curdle.

Pour the custard through a sieve into a mixing bowl. Place in the large basin of ice water and continue whisking until the mixture is cold.

Empty into the prepared ice cream maker and churn until the ice cream is smooth and creamy. Fold in the sticky, poached figs, place into an ice cream container and store in the freezer.

NOTE: To poach the figs, roughly tear the dried figs and place in a small saucepan with 250 ml (1 cup) water, 2 tablespoons brown sugar, 1 tablespoon rum and 1 tablespoon lemon juice. Bring to the boil, then lower the heat to simmer until the figs are very soft and the poaching liquid has turned syrupy, slightly sticky and a glistening deep golden colour. You may have to add another tablespoon or more water if it dries up too much.

We Love Cookies!

I love my cookies, particularly homemade ones with lots of dried fruit! I used to bake them for family and friends in my early teens during the Chinese New Year and Christmas periods. Mom bakes the best ice-block cookies and I've included one of her recipes in this section of the book. It's important to ensure cookies are stored well in a tightly sealed container or jar to maintain freshness.

Fruit, Nut and Oat Cookies

MAKES 44

These are undoubtedly our favourite cookies at home. Yes, there is butter and sugar in them but the oats, dried fruit and nuts make them feel super healthy! You can add any dried fruit you like and omit the walnuts if you're really not a walnut person.

250 g (8.8 oz) unsalted butter, softened at room temperature
165 g (¾ cup) light brown sugar
1 egg
1½ teaspoons vanilla extract
1 teaspoon ground cinnamon
300 g (2 cups) plain flour
200 g (2 cups) rolled oats
300 g (2 cups) mixed dried cranberries, raisins, figs and apricots, roughly chopped into small bits
50 g (½ cup) walnut kernels, toasted

Preheat your oven to 180°C (356°F). Line two baking sheets with greaseproof paper.

In an electric mixer, cream the butter and sugar until pale and fluffy. Add the egg and beat until well combined. Beat in the vanilla. Add the flour and cinnamon and pulse until combined. Include the oats, dried fruit and nuts and pulse until just combined. It might feel like there are a lot of oats but don't worry, it'll all come together.

Roll into 3 cm (1.2 in) balls and place on the baking sheet. Press down gently with a fork and bake for 20 minutes or until lightly golden. Remove from the oven and cool on a wire rack.

Peanut Cookies

MAKES 60

Pop these little morsels in your mouth and they should melt instantly. You'll see these stacked up in shops during the Chinese New Year season in Singapore. I sometimes replace the peanuts with ground almonds or cashews! Give it a go, they are so quick and easy to make!

200 g (7 oz) raw peanuts, roasted in the oven, cooled and ground
200 g (⁴/₅ cup) plain flour
100 g (¹/₂ cup) caster sugar
Pinch of salt
6¹/₂ tablespoons vegetable oil
Roasted peanuts, halved, allow one half per cookie
1 egg, lightly beaten, for glazing

Preheat your oven to 170°C (338°F). Line a baking sheet with greaseproof paper.

Place the peanuts, flour, sugar and salt in a food processor and blitz for 30 seconds. Add the oil and pulse until it forms a dough.

Shape into 2 cm (0.8 in) balls and place onto the baking sheet. Top each with half a peanut, brush with egg wash and bake for 15-20 minutes.

NOTE: The amount of oil required will depend on your climate. In warmer climates, you may not need as much oil. If using icing sugar, 80 g (²/₃ cup) is sufficient. To avoid over blending and getting a pasty dough when blitzing the peanuts, add a couple of tablespoons of sugar and pulse until fine.

Crystalised Ginger, Apricot and Pineapple Cookies

MAKES ABOUT 80

For as long as I can remember, Mom has always experimented with different flavours of cookies using this base recipe. This combo came about when she was given some beautiful dried pineapple and ginger by a friend. The apricot just added a touch of colour and tartness which was perfect. It was quite timely that I visited Singapore a day or two after she had made a batch of these. Within a couple of days, the cookie jar was empty! You can easily make the dough ahead of time, keep it in the fridge and slice to bake when you are ready. These are quick to make and bake, which makes it the perfect recipe!

525 g (3½ cups) plain flour
½ teaspoon baking powder
¼ teaspoon bicarbonate of soda
Pinch of salt
250 g (8.8 oz) unsalted butter, softened at room temperature
150 g (¾ cup) caster sugar
2 eggs
1 large lemon, zest
180 g (1½ cups) chopped crystalised ginger
180 g (1½ cups) chopped dried pineapple
180 g (1½ cups) chopped apricots

Sift the flour, baking powder, bicarbonate of soda and salt into a mixing bowl.

In an electric cake mixer, cream the butter and sugar until pale and fluffy. Add the eggs one at a time, beating well after each addition. Beat in the lemon zest. Add the flour and pulse until a dough is almost formed. Add the dried fruit and pulse until just combined.

Tip the dough onto a lightly floured surface and form into two 30 cm x 5 cm (12 in x 2 in) rectangular logs. Wrap with cling film and refrigerate for at least 30 minutes or until the dough firms up.

Preheat your oven to 180°C (356°F). Line two baking sheets with greaseproof paper.

Dust a sharp knife with flour and cut the dough into 7 mm (0.3 in) thick slices. Place onto the baking sheet, leaving an inch between the cookies and bake for 15 minutes or until the cookie is slightly coloured and cooked through.

Cool on a wire rack and store in an airtight container.

NOTE: If you can find non-sugared crystalised ginger, the cookies will no doubt be less sweet!

Mary Foster's Moonies (Kolac)

MAKES ABOUT 40

Mary is one of my best mate's mother-in-law and she has got to be one of the loveliest women I have ever met in my life. I met Mary some 12 years ago and every visit by me to see their family in Melbourne was like visiting home! The warmth and love that she extended to me and my family, and that she has for her children and grand-children, is unconditional and uncompromising. And like most mothers, she shows it through her love for cooking.

These beautiful Croatian cookies are what she makes frequently for family gatherings. Needless to say, I didn't stop at just one the first time I had them.

It is incredibly apt for me to end this book with Mary's precious recipe of Kolac that everyone so loves. So here it is, from one generation to another, from one family to another, from Mary to me and to you.

250 g (8.8 oz) unsalted butter, softened at room temperature
125 g (1 cup) icing sugar
1 egg
1 teaspoon finely grated orange rind
1½ tablespoons marsala or brandy
300 g (2 cups) self-raising flour
120 g (1 cup) unblanched almonds, chopped
Icing sugar for dusting

Preheat your oven to 160°C (320°F). Line an oven tray with baking paper.

In an electric mixer, cream the butter and sugar until light and creamy. Add the egg, rind and marsala or brandy. Beat well. Fold in the flour and almonds until combined.

Divide the dough into about 40 pieces. To form crescents, roll each piece into 7 cm (about 3 in) logs, curve into a crescent and place on the baking tray. Bake for 12 to 15 minutes or until light golden. Dust with icing sugar while still warm and then again before serving.

NOTE: In temperate climates, divide the cookie dough into equal pieces and refrigerate before forming into crescents. It might help to dab each dough with a little flour, but use sparingly, please!

216

MY FAVOURITE
KITCHEN TOOLS

Kitchen Shears
A good pair of kitchen shears is absolutely essential. I have two, one that allows me to cut through chicken bones and the other is an old school pair of Chinese scissors with a finer tip. They both come in handy!

Knives
Most people purchase an entire knife range. My essentials are simply a chef's knife, a serrated knife, a paring knife and a cleaver! Before you purchase a knife, try it out at the store to ensure it has a comfortable grip and weight to suit you.

Microplane graters
I can't live without my microplane graters. Purchase a fine grater for zesting or grating spices such as nutmeg, and a coarser one for a slightly larger grate. They also come in handy for mincing garlic and ginger and grating hard cheeses like parmesan and pecorino.

Mortar and Pestle
These form one of my prized kitchen utensils. I use it for thumping spice pastes, grinding down toasted dried spices and nuts. It also comes in really handy for making pesto! I prefer those with a deeper bowl to avoid the ingredients from falling out.

Salad Spinner
When I first bought my salad spinner, I wasn't all that convinced that I would use it a lot. It was one of those "nice to have but really didn't need" items. However, it has become one of my treasured items in the kitchen. You might think that giving veggies and herbs a wash and flick is all they need to remove excess water. Well, try spinning it in a salad spinner and see how much excess water you can actually extract. There is nothing worse than a watered down salad or stir-fry!

Silicone spatula

A good silicone spatula with a flexible surface will come in handy for scraping clean a bowl of cake mix to cleaning out curry from a pot! Make sure you have one large and one small for savoury and sweet. There's nothing worse than having your whipped cream tasting of curry!

Steamers

Multi-stacked Chinese steamers are incredibly useful in the kitchen for steaming multiple dishes. I absolutely love mine for steaming my Chinese pork buns and dumplings. They are easy to clean and come in various sizes.

Tweezers

Just when you need them, you realise you don't have them. Tweezers are essential in the kitchen particularly when you are deboning fish or removing tiny little feather stumps on poultry. Most importantly, they enable you to do this whilst keeping intact the flesh of the fish.

Wok

If you are going to own a wok, head down to your nearest Chinatown or Asian grocery store that stock equipment to purchase one. The carbon steel ones conduct heat quickly and allow good searing of meats. They are a good weight and give your dishes just that bit of "wok" flavour. Woks need a little extra care with periodic seasoning. Do this by scrubbing it clean, wiping the inside with vegetable oil using paper towels. Wipe off excess oil with clean towels and heat over medium heat for 15-20 minutes. Keep it dry to avoid rusting. Mom's wok is more than 40 years old. It is so well seasoned that the inside is entirely non-stick whilst the outside is nicely aged and blackened.

Wooden citrus squeezer

These are sometimes called lemon reamers. They are really effective for juicing lemons, limes and oranges.

TIPS AND TRICKS

Temper your spices
Raw spices need to be toasted for the natural oils and flavours to be released. Lightly temper your spices in a dry pan on low-medium heat. You know it is ready when the fragrance permeates the room! Remove from the heat and pan and let it cool before using a mortar and pestle to grind it down.

Blender or mortar and pestle?
I was taught to make spice pastes the traditional way, using the mortar and pestle. Over the years, I've mastered the art of thumping. It comes with relaxing the arm, loosening one's grip and letting the pestle do the job. Start off with thumping the tougher herbs such as galangal and lemongrass, adding to the mix the more tender herbs as you go. The big difference is that the mortar and pestle bruises, hence releases the fragrance of the herbs whilst the blender or food processor cuts the herbs. You generally need to add a little extra liquid when blending or blitzing in a food processor to help it along. Either way, it's important to do what works for you from a quality and time perspective. If you really haven't got the time, then chuck it all in a blender or food processor. But please, ensure you buy one that has blades close to the base or is able to finely grind the ingredients to a paste.

Finely chopped garlic
To peel the skin off garlic easily, place the flat side of your knife over the garlic clove and crush with the heel of your palm. Discard the skin and with your fingers firmly placed over the blunt top edge of your knife, chop finely.

Freezing spice pastes
I'm a big fan of freezing spice pastes in portion sizes. Then, when the craving for a good curry comes along, you can whip it up pretty quickly. Make sure you store them well in an air-tight or vacuum-sealed bag before freezing. Flatten the bag for easy stacking in the freezer. However, there are certain curry paste, such as green curry pastes, that could turn a little bitter once frozen.

Treating vegetables and herbs

I always wash my vegetables prior to using. It is important to ensure all the water is drained before using them. I find using a salad spinner really helps remove excess water. Fresh coriander is notorious for holding onto lots of soil and grit particularly on the stems near the root, so wash these well before using.

Grain fed or grass fed?

There are many schools of thought as to which is better and which is tastier. Like all food, it's a matter of personal taste! I much prefer the flavour of grass-fed beef, just as nature intended.

Marinating meat

For maximum flavour, always allow time to marinate your meat. Some marinades, such as those with ginger, also help tenderise your meat. However, add too much of these and leave it to marinate for a long time can result in mushy meat! So, ensure that these are added in sparingly if the recipe calls for meats to be marinated overnight. Or simply add them into the marinade just a little while before cooking. I always use a glass or ceramic bowl or even a Ziplock plastic bag when marinating meats rather than aluminium or copper-based bowls as marinades that contain acid will react with the surface resulting in an unpleasant metallic undertone or discolouration of your meat.

Don't overcrowd your pan!

You have probably heard this a million times. Well, let's look at a beef stir-fry. The idea is to sear the meat and seal in the juices. So what's required is even, high heat. If you place too much meat and overcrowd your pan, the wonderful juices in the meat will seep out and you'll end up stewing the meat, resulting in toughness. Thus, it is much better to cook your meat in batches for larger servings.

Cooking with pressure cookers

I often use pressure cookers when I'm stretched for time and need to halve my cooking time for meat and soups. However, pressure cooking tends to release much more liquid than slow cooking on the stove. I tend to cook a dish a little less than the prescribed time, and leave the rest of the cooking time with the pressure off or lid off over the stove. This often helps reduce the liquid and creates a richer finish. Get to know your pressure cooker well. If you can, once the cooking time is completed, remove from the heat and allow the pressure to slowly subside. This will happen when the dish cools. If you really need to reduce the pressure quickly, use the pressure release gauge on the cooker or run it under cold water.

Resting the dough

Resting pastry dough allows the gluten to "relax" which makes rolling out pastries much easier and results in less shrinkage when baking.

Cold hands are good for pastries

Cold hands and pastries go hand in hand. If you've always got warm hands, be quick when working with pastries as warm hands very quickly warm up your pastry and makes them difficult to manage. If you are just one of those who can't avoid warm hands, then place the rolled out dough in the fridge to firm up before using.

Rolling out your pastry dough

This is a great tip my mother taught me. Roll your dough out between two clear plastic sheets. It not only makes the whole process of rolling out your dough that much easier with minimum mess, it also maintains the integrity of your dough without having to add additional flour. So, next time you purchase a plastic bag of fruit from the super-market, save some clean ones just for rolling out pastry.

INDEX

EXTRA GOODIES

Audra on TV and the web *I am excited to be one of the three judges on Masterchef Asia. Having been through the experience of Masterchef Australia and now building my own brand in the food business, it's a great opportunity to inspire and mentor. Masterchef Asia screens on Lifetime right across Asia.*

"Tasty Conversations" is my own short-form cooking series produced by the great folks at Carnival Productions in Sydney. I am delighted that this series is broadcasted on Nine's HD GEM in Australia and on fyi broadcasting across Asia. Look out for online versions of this series on http://tastyconversations.com.au. Series 2 features absolutely everything I love about Singaporean food. Some of the recipes included from this book are my mouthwatering Laksa, Nonya Chicken Curry and Raw Salmon with Szechuan Dressing.

Audra's Food Products *I have launched a range of food products utilising the best of Australian seasonal produce with an intent to fully support local growers. Each jar of relish and jam encapsulates my passion for food and pure love of cooking. The range currently includes a Plum Chilli Relish, perfect for dolloping over a juicy beef burger or as a perfect accompaniment to cheeses; a Pickled Green Chilli Mayo which, when smothered in a pulled pork slider, takes you to a very happy place; and finally, my Vanilla Bean Fig Jam which is perfect on top of rye toast, as a topping for a tart, with cheese or just dolloped over your favourite vanilla ice-cream. All my products are natural, free from preservatives and colouring and gluten free. They are currently available at Hubers Butchery at Dempsey in Singapore. For stockists in Australia, please contact info@audramorrice.com.au*

Audra Caters *Food is a way to invigorate the senses, excite the palate and warm the spirit, giving great satisfaction and comfort to your dining experience. This is what my catering is all about.*

I currently cater for both corporate and private-dining events in Sydney, Australia. Inspired largely by my rich cultural heritage from growing up in Singapore and my love for food, I also gather inspiration from my travels and the people I meet.

My specialty dining event, Cook & Feast, is an intimate cooking class coupled with a dining experience where diners not only learn to cook some of my dishes but also learn about their origins and heritage.

Regular pop-up dinners are an ongoing activity featuring my eclectic Asian style of cooking!

For all catering enquiries, please contact info@audramorrice.com.au.